VITAL
CHRISTIANITY

VITAL CHRISTIANITY

THE LIFE AND SPIRITUALITY
OF
WILLIAM WILBERFORCE

MURRAY ANDREW PURA

CLEMENTS PUBLISHING
Toronto
CHRISTIAN FOCUS

ISBN 1 85792 916 0

Published in 2003
by
Christian Focus Publications Ltd.,
Geanies House,
Fearn By Tain, Ross-Shire,
Scotland, UK, IV20 1TW
www.christianfocus.com
and
Clements Publishing
Box 213, 6021 Yonge Street
Toronto, Ontario M2M 3W2 Canada
www.clementspublishing.com

Cover Design by Alister MacInnes
Printed and Bound by
Cox & Wyman, Reading, Berkshire

Contents

For Donald Munro Lewis
teacher, scholar, friend
non verba sed tonitrua

Foreword

Little William Wilberforce, like little John Wesley, his older contemporary, was a great man who impacted the Western world as few others have done. Blessed with brains, charm, influence and initiative, much wealth and fair health (though slightly crippled and with chronic digestive difficulties), he put evangelicalism on Britain's map as a power for social change, first by overthrowing the slave trade almost single-handed and then by generating a stream of societies for doing good and reducing evil in national life. Beside his own track record as a visionary in Parliament, he became more than anyone else the architect of mainstream nineteenth-century evangelical Anglicanism, just as Wesley, the visionary shepherd of religious societies, became the main architect of nineteenth-century worldwide Methodism. To forget such men is foolish; their lives need to be written afresh for each new generation. In the last century Coupland and Pollock, among others, wrote well of Wilberforce's public life, and now comes Murray Andrew Pura's brief but well-judged portrayal of the man himself and his personal style. I welcome this work, for Pura's picking up of the important things about Wilberforce and the wisdom he lived by is insightful and inspiring.

British evangelical piety in the eighteenth and nineteenth centuries was essentially Puritan piety, as taught by seventeenth-century pundits like Baxter and Owen and Bunyan, and by their faithful next-century disciples, Philip Doddridge, Jonathan Edwards, John Newton and other such. Pura shows how the writings of these men, plus personal ministry from Isaac Milner, Newton and others, shaped Wilberforce's faith and devotion. We learn how wrong we would be to suppose that any of these men expected sound conversions to be sudden, as moderns tend to do, and also how wrong Wilberforce's sons were to imply in their biography of him that his distinctive evangelicalism faded at the end of his life, as their own had done. On all aspects of Wilberforce's "vital Christianity" Pura is a sure guide.

Some books, said Bacon, should be tasted (and then left), some swallowed (that is, read casually), and "some few chewed and digested," that is read through with care and thought. This book flows so smoothly that it could easily be swallowed, but with Christian role-models of stature currently in such short supply I believe it belongs in Bacon's third class; and it is as such that I recommend it to you.

J. I. Packer
Board of Governors' Professor of Theology
Regent College

Acknowledgments

The core of this book was established fifteen years ago. For that I must thank the encouragement and wisdom of Donald M. Lewis who oversaw my thesis work from start to finish. I must also thank the librarians of both Regent College and the Vancouver School of Theology in Vancouver, British Columbia, Canada for their kind assistance. That it sees the light of day in its present incarnation is due to the hard work and expertise of my editor, Rob Clements. I am grateful for his belief in this work and in his persistence in ensuring it saw publication.

CHAPTER I

William Wilberforce
An Introduction

By the time of his death in 1833, William Wilberforce had exerted a tremendous influence on English society, an influence which would extend well beyond his own generation. His impact was such that one historian, Ford K. Brown, has termed his period "The Age of Wilberforce."[1] Indeed, his political involvements and his leadership in the fledgling Anglican Evangelical Movement have caused Brown to contend that he, not John Wesley, deserves the credit for the moral reformation that swept Britain.[2] These are not idle claims. Wilberforce was a man very much involved with social change. It was his concern that Great Britain become holy and he set out to make her so. He not only fought slavery and the slave trade but also worked for penal reform and for changes in a British criminal code which he considered inhumane. He desired education and medical treatment for the poor. He wanted laws to protect children employed in factories and as chimney sweeps. He wished to see Sunday respected as a Christian Sabbath. He hoped that the Christian scriptures would be distributed throughout the British Empire. He worked to establish Christian missionaries in India. There was no aspect of British life or influence that he did not want to see affected by the Christian gospel.

Christianity had changed him, and he knew it could change society.

William Wilberforce certainly would have maintained that the greatest single influence on his life was his religious faith and it is with this presupposition that this writer approaches his subject. In the words of the late Sir Reginald Coupland, Beit Professor of Colonial History at Oxford University, Wilberforce's religious faith was the "secret of Wilberforce's indomitable perseverance," bracing him "for the business of the active world outside."[3] Ernest Howse has argued that Wilberforce's deeds of social reform were "inspired almost wholly by motives of pietistic origin."[4] James Houston has asserted: "The main credit for the abolition of the slave trade belongs to William Wilberforce. Behind that lay his consuming desire to manifest real Christianity."[5] It is axiomatic that the motivation for such an influential life ought to be studied, and if that motivation lies in a man's religious faith and thought then these ought to be understood.

Wilberforce, while raised an Anglican, underwent a conversion experience at the age of twenty-six and embraced an Evangelical understanding of the Christian faith which he championed to his dying day.[6] He became the most important leader of Evangelical Anglicanism and sought to commend a moderate and cultured version of evangelicalism to Britain's middle and upper classes. To understand his faith is in some large measure to understand early Evangelicalism. It is the purpose of this biography to examine the influences upon Wilberforce's spiritual development and to assess their importance. It will also seek to demonstrate how his spirituality affected his personal life, his political commitments, and his social consciousness, and thus, in turn, influenced Wilberforce's world. It may be that here, at an early stage of the Evangelical Movement, something of evangelicalism's true soul can be rediscovered.

A Definition of Spirituality

Spirituality is a term used to describe how an individual or group relates to God as God is conceived to be. It is concerned primarily with how humans are to commune with God through prayer and worship. Inevitably, however, these concerns become all-inclusive as every aspect of a person's life is brought into relationship with God. Spirituality asks, "How is one to understand and out of this understanding live a life of communion with God?" This "life of communion" ought to be outlined in the broadest terms, not just in respect to verbal prayer or formal worship in a sanctuary.

"How is one to understand and out of this understanding live a life of communion with God?" This same question can be asked by the Buddhist, the Muslim, and the Christian, but the answers will not be the same. Indeed, among different groups within the Christian consensus the answers will not be the same. Therefore the application of the term "spirituality" to any individual or group implies specificity. The definition of spirituality as the way in which one communes with God with the whole of one's life remains the same. The difference lies in the manner and the quality of that all-inclusive communion.

A Definition of Wilberforce's Evangelical Spirituality

Once William Wilberforce became converted to the Christian faith, a particular Christian spirituality began to develop within him which increasingly reshaped his personal life and his political commitments. It arose out of the teachings of the Evangelical Movement, a group within the Anglican Church of which Wilberforce became a key figure.

In embracing an Evangelical understanding of the Christian faith Wilberforce had inherited two spiritual traditions, one rather older and the other quite new. The older spiritual tradition was that of the sixteenth century Reformation. In fact, "evangelical" was the earliest word in English for adherents of that Reformation.[7] According to Donald G. Bloesch:

> In its historical meaning evangelical has come to refer to the kind of religion espoused by the Protestant Reformation. It is also associated with the spiritual movements of purification subsequent to the Reformation—Pietism and Puritanism. The revival movements within Protestantism in the eighteenth and nineteenth centuries have also been appropriately termed evangelical.[8]

The newer spiritual tradition Wilberforce fell heir to was that of the Evangelical Movement, comprised of those influenced by the eighteenth century Evangelical (or Methodist) Revival who chose to remain, like John Wesley and George Whitefield, within the Established Church, as opposed to the movement of evangelical Dissent (and eventually of Methodism) which consisted of those who felt that to remain within the Established Church was to compromise their Christian faith.[9] These two movements of evangelicalism shared a mutual animosity for one another. Many Anglican Evangelicals felt that evangelical Dissent damaged the cause of Christ in Britain. Wilberforce wrote in the fall of 1789, four years after his conversion, that "the increase of dissenters, which always follow from the institution of unsteepled places of worship, is highly injurious to the interests of religion in the long run."[10] By the end of the eighteenth century Anglican Evangelicalism had distanced itself from both evangelical Dissent and Methodism (which had by then cut ties with the Church of England).[11] It did so because Dissent and Methodism were both politically suspect, because Dissent was hostile to the Church of England and Methodism was expected to become so, and because Anglican Evangelicals wished to be viewed as legitimate and loyal members of the Church of England. W.J.C. Ervine comments: "It was…expedient for Anglican Evangelicalism to dissociate itself from all taint of 'novelty,' 'enthusiasm,' or political non-conformity, and to strengthen the movement's Anglican pedigree."[12] Therefore the Evangelical Movement's periodical, *The Christian Observer*, retained an Anglican flavor and usually ignored the activities of evangelical Dissent, a number of Anglican Evangelical and Dissenting (or Nonconformist) clergy saw themselves in distinct rivalry with one another, and the Anglican Evangelicals preferred to start up their own missionary society with an Anglican orientation rather than support the London Missionary Society which was founded along Dissenting lines.[13]

Nevertheless, Anglican Evangelicalism and evangelical Dissent still had common roots. Both were rooted in that older spiritual tradition of the Protestant Reformation and shared its theological and spiritual distinctives: the supreme authority of Scripture, *sola scriptura*, salvation by grace alone, *sola gratia*, through faith alone, *sola fide*, in Christ alone, *sola Christus*. Moreover, both were rooted in eighteenth century evangelicalism and, theoretically at least, Anglican Evangelicals could not sever themselves completely from their Dissenting brothers and sisters, for they themselves "firmly held that ultimate truth did not lie in one Church order or another, but in the gospel itself."[14] Thus, the British and Foreign Bible Society, which Wilberforce played a major role in founding, became one area of strong co-operation between the two evangelical factions.[15] This theological stance cost Anglican Evangelicals a great deal in terms of abuse from and unpopularity with Anglican High-Churchmen, but they did not change their minds about it.[16]

As an Anglican Evangelical, therefore, Wilberforce developed a spirituality basically consistent with the sacramental claims of Anglicanism, as well as with the spiritual claims of the Protestant Reformation, particularly the English Reformers, which were imbedded in eighteenth century British evangelicalism. What made Evangelical spirituality especially distinctive in this period was its particular emphases in the areas of soteriology and pneumatology. "Evangelicalism centred upon soteriology," states Doreen M. Rosman, "and its soteriology centred upon the Cross."[17] Thus in 1811 Charles Simeon, the most influential of all Evangelical clergymen, entitled a university address, "Christ crucified, or evangelical religion described," and proposed that the description "evangelical" could only properly be applied to those who like St. Paul "determined not to know anything among you save Jesus Christ and him crucified."[18] The work of the Holy Spirit was considered crucial both in the salvation of the human soul and in the Christian's ongoing spiritual growth: "This emphasis upon the activity of the Spirit...most obviously differentiated evangelicals' beliefs from those of their fellows."[19] These spiritual distinctives Anglican Evangelicals shared with evangelical Dissent. What particularly differentiated the spirituality of the two evangelical groups in this context was the fact that most Anglican Evangelicals played down any teaching stipulating the crucial nature of a violent and sudden personal conversion experience, whereas evangelical Dissent and Methodism played this up.[20]

William Wilberforce was both a loyal Anglican and a staunch Evangelical. Anglican Evangelicalism formed the hub around which every aspect of Wilberforce's religious life turned. By virtue of the fact that his relationship with God affected everything else he did, this Evangelicalism also influenced all the activities of his extremely busy life. Everything centred on Wilberforce's redemption from eternal damnation by Christ's sacrificial death at Calvary. All was seen in light of the work of the Holy Spirit who labored daily to make the reality of that redemption part of Wilberforce's personal experience. Wilberforce shared these spiritual emphases with thousands of other Evangelicals both in England and overseas. The hallmarks of his religious life and thought, they were the mainsprings to his political career.

Notes

1. Ford K. Brown, *Fathers of the Victorians* (Cambridge: Cambridge University Press, 1961), p. 4.

2. Ibid.

3. Reginald Coupland, *Wilberforce* (Collins, 1923), p. 190.

4. Ernest Howse, *Saints in Politics* (Toronto: University of Toronto, 1952), p. 182.

5. James Houston, ed., *Real Christianity* (Portland: Multnomah Press, 1982), p. xii.

6. Wilberforce's sons and some historians, such as Brown and Robin Furneaux, claim otherwise. They argue that in his later years Wilberforce turned increasingly to the High Church Anglicanism. The issue will be discussed at the end of Chapter III.

7. G. R. Balleine, *A History of the Evangelical Party in the Church of England* (London: Longmans, Green, and Co., 1911), p. 37.

8. Donald G. Bloesch, *Essentials of Evangelical Theology*, 2 vols. (San Francisco: Harper & Row, 1978-9), 1:7.

9. Balleine, p. 37. Though the term "Methodist Revival" has often been used in conjunction with the revival sparked by the preaching of George Whitefield and John Wesley, "Evangelical Revival" is closer to the truth since not every person affected by the revival became a

Methodist. The use of *Evangelical* with a capital *E* will be used to denote Anglican Evangelicals, while evangelical with a small *e* will denote its generic use unless accompanied by the term Dissent or Dissenting. This is in conformity with standard academic practice in this field.

10. William Wilberforce, quoted in Robert Isaac Wilberforce and Samuel Wilberforce, *The Life of William Wilberforce*, 5 vols. (London: John Murray, 1838), 1:248.

11. William Joseph Clydesdale Ervine, "Doctrine and Diplomacy: some aspects of the life and thought of the Anglican Evangelical clergy, 1797-1837" (Ph.D. thesis, University of Cambridge, 1979), p. 27.

12. Ibid., p. 26.

13. Ibid., pp. 29-30

14. Ibid., p. 29.

15. Ibid., p.30

16. Ibid.

17. Doreen M. Rosman, *Evangelicals and Culture* (London and Canberra: Croom Helm, 1984), p. 10.

18. Ibid.

19. Ibid., pp. 11-12

20. Elisabeth Jay, *The Religion of the Heart* (Oxford: Clarendon Press, 1979), p. 60.

CHAPTER II

The Historical Setting
An Overview of Conditions in Great Britain

The Political Situation

William Wilberforce's influence on the course of British politics and British society was pronounced during his career. Brown argues that it was the Evangelicals under William Wilberforce's leadership who were responsible for the moral improvement of England, not John Wesley and his Methodists.[1] The latter laid a foundation which Wilberforce expanded on, leading particularly lay Evangelicals in the Church of England in a reform movement that became immense and well-organized. Wilberforce's example led many into influential areas of public service. Moreover, the Anglican Evangelicals had connections with the ruling class which allowed them to infiltrate this crucial sector of society with the Christian gospel and its demands—this, according to Brown, was the secret of their success.[2] However, it was Wilberforce who made it possible, through the example he set in the use of his occupation for Christ, his organization of dozens of private groups for the aid of society, and the publication of his book, *A Practical View of the Prevailing Religious System of Professed Christians*, which along with William Law's *A Serious Call* and Philip Doddridge's

The Rise and Progress of Religion in the Soul formed the block of literature most critical for Evangelicalism's direction and development "An important factor," says Brown, "of the Evangelicals' success…was simply Wilberforce's incomparable leadership."[3] His place in the period as a politician, a reformer, as a personality, and as a Christian is pre-eminent.

William Wilberforce grew up in an England striving to consolidate herself as a world power. The year of his birth, 1759, was the year British forces defeated the French on the Plains of Abraham and took possession of Canada, a crucial victory of the Seven Years' War in which Britain (and Prussia) triumphed in 1763. Wars raged throughout his lifetime. As a young man of seventeen, Wilberforce sat in the gallery of the House of Commons and listened to the debates concerning the war with the American colonies which had begun in 1775. Britain lost the colonies in 1783 and had to fight another war against them in 1812, managing to quell American attempts to capture territory from the British in Canada.

In 1789, the French Revolution brought down France's monarchy and created a republic which went to war with Britain in 1793. For the next twenty-two years, during both the Revolutionary Wars with the French Republic as well as the Napoleonic Wars, Britain proved to be the major sea power. However, English forces were not nearly as successful on land. Napoleon Bonaparte plagued Britain and her allies throughout his military career.

Coming on the scene in 1796, Napoleon became the First Consul of France in 1799 after a coup which toppled the corrupt Revolutionary government. In 1804, he became Emperor and ruled for ten years, defeating every European coalition set up to oppose him on the battlefield and establishing a considerable continental empire. Even with her powerful naval squadrons England lived in fear of a French invasion. Napoleon was finally defeated at Leipzig in 1813, and though he escaped from exile and ruled as Emperor during the Hundred Days, combined British and Prussian forces shattered Napoleon's army at Waterloo in 1815. At this point Britain achieved a peace from extensive military involvement which endured for many years.

By the time Wilberforce was elected MP for York in 1784 he was already close friends with William Pitt the Younger who became Prime Minister in 1783 at the age of twenty-four. Both shared a zeal for seeing reform within England and her colonies and it was Pitt who, when Wilberforce became dangerously ill and could not be present in Parliament, moved the investigation of the Slave Trade in 1788. Although Wilberforce's conversion to Christianity in 1785 tempered their friendship, the two remained close until Pitt's death in 1806. Wilberforce supported many of Pitt's fiscal and tariff reforms, voting against him only rarely on matters of Christian conscience.

Wilberforce, who was a Tory, worked with the governments of a number of Prime Ministers, as well as with several monarchs. Pitt was Prime Minister from 1783-1801, at which point his disagreement with George III over Catholic Emancipation caused his resignation. Henry Addington became the Prime Minister from 1801-4. Pitt then regained his office and led the government until his death. But both Addington and, astonishingly, Pitt, had become cool to Wilberforce's campaign for the abolition of the British slave trade, and Pitt's death actually opened the way for the end of the trade under the coalition government of William Grenville. Spencer Perceval, an Evangelical of whom Wilberforce was fond, became Prime Minister in 1809, but was assassinated in 1812, at which point Robert Banks Liverpool formed a government which became known for its repressive measures. In 1822, Robert Peel and George Canning began to bring more liberal legislation before the House. Canning actually became Prime Minister for four months in 1827. At his death Frederick John Robinson (Goderich) led the country until the Duke of Wellington became Prime Minister in 1828, three years after Wilberforce retired from politics. It was the Whig administration of Charles Grey that, in 1833, carried the bill which ended slavery in the British Empire.

The three English monarchs who ruled during Wilberforce's life and career were George III, George IV, and William IV. George III began his reign in 1760, when Wilberforce was a year old, and carried on until 1820, although his son, George IV, acted as regent after 1811 when his father became insane. George IV became actual king in 1820 and remained on the throne until 1830, when his brother William IV, the third son of George III, took over the monarchy until 1837.

George III opposed the abolition of the slave trade and was suspicious of Wilberforce. His son George IV was an unpopular monarch due to his support of Liverpool's repressive measures (especially the use of military force at a peaceful meeting of fifty thousand people at St. Peter's Field in 1819), as well as his attempt to divorce Queen Caroline. William IV was no more of a reformer than his father or his brother on the issue of slavery, and as Duke of Clarence in 1807 he defended the status of the slave trade during the debate on abolition in the House of Lords.

Many of Wilberforce's attempts at legislation for social improvement were frustrated by a prevailing fear of Jacobinism in England, a concern that the kind of radical politics which had destroyed the monarchy and aristocracy in France would sweep through English society as well. This caused all sorts of restraints and interfered with social and parliamentary reform. Even Wilberforce himself, because of his dread of revolution in England, voted for some of these restraints: under Pitt, the so-called Gagging Bills against seditious meetings and practices, as well as the Combination Acts, which prohibited the formation of trade unions; under Liverpool, the suspension of *habeas corpus*.

This increased his unpopularity with those desiring radical political change, persons who were already unhappy with Wilberforce because of his conservative views and, in their eyes, his lack of concern for the "white wage slaves" of England's factories and mills. They saw him not as a reformer but as an obstacle to reform since his manner of bringing about social changed included influencing the great, patronizing nobility, and accommodating his reform to both groups.[4]

But Wilberforce did not oppose the good the Radicals wished to do, only the means they were apparently ready to use to achieve it. Wilberforce was not a democrat. He conceived of society as designed hierarchically and organically by God—all parts were to work together as they were defined, and the leaders in society were to rule and to guide as well as help the weak and the poor (who were also to know and keep their particular place in God's design.) Wilberforce, along with the other Evangelicals of the eighteenth century, was a paternalist, and he spoke out against democracy because it upset God's hierarchical structure for society. He was for social change in terms of making things better, but he was not in favor of a complete alteration of society. So when political radicals, like William Cobbett, spread the teachings of the Enlightenment among the working classes, Wilberforce saw them as fomenting rebellion against the British Constitution and government as well as against God. He feared the same bloodbath and demise of religion which the Enlightenment had brought to France. Therefore he supported repressive legislation during his career.

Yet he subscribed to Cobbett's paper, considered him "a very able and influential teacher,"[5] (even though the "enlightened" Cobbett supported the slave trade), and initially backed Robert Owen's socialist theories until Owen began to blatantly attack religion. Their disavowal of Christianity caused the greatest breach between Wilberforce and the Radicals, for he could not see the value of material and intellectual advancement if the moral condition of the populace was left to fend for itself without the Christian faith. So he opposed Cobbett, Percy Bysshe Shelley, and William Hazlitt, but supported Christian reformers like James Montgomery and Michael Sadler.

Much of the social reform which did occur during Wilberforce's lifetime did not come about through political process, but through private individuals and organizations independent of the government. Certainly Wilberforce was able to bring about many of the changes he desired in English society through the use of his own money and by means of the numerous groups he set up to deal with the problems he considered particularly pressing. His vision was for a Christian nation, a vision garnered from the Old Testament concepts of Israel as a holy nation, as well as from writings of the English Puritans who had pursued this same vision in the seventeenth century. The concept had also come up through Augustine, a great favorite of the Calvinist Reformers and the Calvinist Puritans, who, in *The City of God*, asserted that "government without God ends in aimless and bloody chaos, and that, conversely, man has it in his power corporately to create the Good Society under God."[6] This is the society which Wilberforce and the Clapham Group sought to produce. They were encouraged in their endeavors by the post-millennial optimism of the period which taught them that Christ would return to rule the earth after one thousand years of universal peace and spiritual success.[7] Why should not this millennium of righteousness begin due to the influence of a holy Britain and a holy Empire and why should not the Evangelicals be God's instruments and means of bringing this about?

Wilberforce did not seek to create a holy nation through means of violence, as in the establishment of the French Republic, nor did he mean to see it produced by a restructuring of British society, as the Radicals hoped to bring about. Wilberforce felt that he must work in and through that structure to bring about God's desired society. Thus, in the age of polarization, Wilberforce was neither radical nor ultra-conservative but a moderate who avoided party allegiance and preferred to operate as a political independent. He did this in order to be free to act according to what he perceived to be the will of God and to be in line with the dictates of his own Evangelical Christian conscience.

The Economic and Social Situation

The England of Wilberforce was full of as much economic and social turmoil as political. It was changing into an industrial nation. The Industrial Revolution began soon after Wilberforce's birth and continued throughout his lifetime, lasting about sixty years.[8] New inventions such as the flying shuttle, the spinning jenny, and the steam engine helped bring about greater productivity in the textile and iron industries. Those who owned these new means of production and the factories in which the goods were produced on a mass scale became as wealthy as England's landed aristocracy. The Industrial Revolution gave the middle class a new prominence and influence on the English social and political scene. However, this Revolution also added enormously to England's social problems.

Women and children were exploited by many factory owners as a means of cheap labor. Population increase and urbanization resulted in the cities growing at such a pace that improperly built housing was thrown up—factory workers existed under living arrangements that soon developed into slum conditions. The Agricultural Revolution which resulted in the loss of farms and farm animals displaced the smaller English farmer so that even more people flooded the cities looking for work. Often as many as ten or twelve persons were living in the same tiny apartment in the poorer sections of the cities; rural conditions were no less crowded, three or four families often crammed into the same bedroom in counties throughout England.[9]

The cities spawned poverty for the workers while they spawned wealth for the factory owners. Children could not be fed and infanticide resulted.[10] Women who could not tolerate factory conditions, or who could not find work, resorted to prostitution. There grew to be thirty to fifty thousand prostitutes in and around London alone, one-in-four of the population of single women.[11] Juvenile prostitution also developed as abandoned children struggled desperately to survive. Girls between the ages of eleven and fourteen were involved, while young boys turned to petty crime and joined gangs which consisted of twenty or thirty of them at a time.[12] The criminal code which dealt with these children was harsh. There were 160 hanging offenses, often for the most trivial of crimes, and children were routinely subjected to the severe and degenerate conditions of England's jails and prisons throughout the period of Wilberforce's career. As late as 1818 he was being told about the sodomy that young boys were victims of in the prisons and a visit to Newgate with Elizabeth Fry confirmed to him that many children were incarcerated "with the refuse of society."[13]

The Revolutionary and Napoleonic wars brought income to those producing uniforms and munitions, but the large number of soldiers and sailors increased the amount of violence in English society. Military personnel were often demoralized and brutal, not surprising when it is taken into consideration that a good number were physically forced into military service by press gangs. Violence and crime were not easily controlled in England as the only location in which there was paid police was London. In fact, the government did not support a public police force, any sort of public health program, or any public education.[14] One thing which the poor could get ahold of in ample quantities, however, was cheap gin, so that alcoholism also became a part of the depressed conditions.

Shipowners in England gained new wealth off the misfortunes of Africans sold as slaves to the West Indies plantation owners. Slaving by British ships existed at least as early as the time of Elizabeth I,[15] but the "boom decade" was 1783-1793 when Liverpool ships alone took 303, 737 Africans to the West Indies, selling them for over fifteen million pounds.[16] London, Bristol, and Liverpool were engaged in the slave trade, but by the time of the Revolutionary war with France, Liverpool controlled more than half of all the British trade and almost half of Europe's.[17] The trade was brisk up to the very end. In 1806-7, just before the slave trade was ended in the British Empire, 185 British ships forced 43,755 Africans into slavery on the West Indies' plantations.[18] Those opposed to the Abolition of the Trade which came in 1807 predicted dire economic consequences for England, but these predictions never came true, except perhaps that those engaged in the traffic got no richer than they had become.

Such were the social conditions Wilberforce fought to change. Many of these problems were not dealt with because of the numerous wars and the drain they made on the government's resources. There was the fast and confusing rush of the Industrial Revolution where the owners of the factories saw themselves as a benefit, not a curse, to the community. There was also their greed. There was the theology, some of which Wilberforce subscribed to, which taught people to believe that poverty was good for the soul: "Workingmen were expected to remain patient under affliction and look forward for better days to heaven alone."[19] Helping the poor was considered to be a duty of the wealthy, not the government. Here Wilberforce was again exemplary, giving anywhere from a quarter to a third of his income away for purposes of social improvement (and this does not include the considerable funds he poured into religious causes.)[20] But few, including the generous Evangelical philanthropists, had any concept of social justice. Wilberforce and the majority of his generation were locked into those economic policies set down by the Scot Adam Smith in his book *The Wealth of Nations* which was published in 1776.

Smith's influential book advocated free trade and private enterprise and opposed any kind of state interference in a nation's economic process. This was the inception of the system of ideas known as *laissez faire* through which capitalism grew. As taught by Smith, it assumed rational laws that governed economic activity. Jack C. Estrin states:

> Men left alone to pursue selfish ends in the use of their capital and labor would ultimately produce social good. The laws of free trade and of competition, of supply and demand, would determine success and failure in the economic struggle for existence; but the end result would be an increase in the total national wealth.[21]

England was the only country which followed this doctrine to the letter.[22] *Laissez faire* did accomplish miracles in production in England through the Industrial Revolution, but it has already been noted that this Revolution caused widespread suffering as well. The poor who had scant opportunity to amass capital and thus profit under the system scarcely benefited from the new-found prosperity of others unless this came about through acts of charity or philanthropy. With the formation of trade unions seen as conspiracy and the rule that the state must not interfere with the economic process instigated by "selfish men" in the numerous mills and factories, very little could be done to see to it that laborers were properly paid and properly treated. Wilberforce and the Evangelicals tried to alleviate this suffering, but to have attempted to alter the entire system which spawned such abuse would have been rebellious in their eyes.

All of the above factors mitigated against widespread social change, yet considerable improvement had occurred by Wilberforce's death on account of his activities and leadership of the Evangelical Movement. He worked for the improvement of the morality of English society by forming the Society for the Reformation of Manners. He supported Elizabeth Fry and Samuel Romilly in their effort for penal reform and contributed to the efforts to humanize the English criminal code. Medical aid for the poor was important to him. So was the use of children in chimney sweeping and in factories—he helped push an act through Parliament limiting the hours children worked in the new cotton mills of northern England, and he supported the Society for Bettering the Condition and Increasing the Comforts of the Poor, as well as founding the Climbing Boy Society, two organizations which tried to help the children employed as chimney sweeps.[23] Wilberforce also championed popular education, especially education for the poor and deaf, at a time when even political radicals like Cobbett scorned the concept.[24] He approved of Catholic Emancipation before his reform-minded friend William Pitt, desiring admission of Catholics to a united Parliament as early as 1798.[25] Despite the limitations which paternalism and the economics of Adam Smith placed upon Wilberforce and the Evangelicals, they were still able to accomplish an enormous amount of good.

The Religious Situation

Before the advent of the Evangelical Revival in England and the subsequent Evangelical Movement of which Wilberforce became a leader, the religious atmosphere of the country was one which strongly emphasized the importance of reason. The eighteenth century was the Age of Reason and Enlightenment.[26] The physics of Isaac Newton (1643-1727) had demonstrated that the universe was perfectly mechanical and material and that the key to understanding it was human reason not divine revelation.[27] The philosophical skepticism of John Locke (1632-1704) clamed that ultimate matter, the quality or substance of what can be sensed externally, would always be unknowable.[28] Therefore, it was pointless to argue over what was the ultimate meaning of things. Instead, reasonableness and compromise ought to be the hallmark of discussions on the significance of the universe in which humans lived.[29] George Berkeley (1685-1753), Irish philosopher and Anglican bishop, expounded a system of subjective idealism in his works. There wasn't any Matter in the universe, he said. Ideas were what counted. Reality was what the Mind perceived according to each individual.[30]

All of this had its influence on Christianity in England. Morality was seen as important, as essential to the reasonable and enlightened man, but even more important, given the teachings of Locke and Berkeley, was the spirit of good-natured compromise. Keith Feiling states:

> It [the Church of England] ceased to think of itself as a divinely-built society, set apart by an apostolic succession, built on revelation and unbroken tradition. The new generation stressed "the reasonableness" of Christianity, for they wished to conciliate it with modern thinking.[31]

The exaltation of reason led to a skepticism toward God and toward the miraculous. With moralism replacing the need for personal redemption by faith in the atoning sacrifice of Christ came the erosion of the sacramental aspects of Anglican Christianity. A small number of intellectuals turned to Unitarianism with its denial of the Trinity and Christ's deity, and its emphasis on reason, character, and conscience as the keys to Christian practice and belief. Other intellectuals were embracing Deism, "a rational compromise between faith and Newtonian physics,"[32] which taught that nature, not Christ and his miracles, was the perfect—and only—revelation of God to humankind. Latitudinarianism was another result of the stress on human reason, expounding anthrocentrism, an inevitable result of making the human mind the measure of all that was right and good.

The consequence of all this for the Church of England was not only a decline in the numbers of its adherents and a disinterest in Christian doctrine by those who did attend, but a toppling of religious standards within the clergy of the Church itself. "Lax morality, mercenary interest and actual bad practice if not moral corruptness"[33] became grim signs of a loss of faith in Christianity's theological distinctives by Anglican bishops and priests. Nor could the strong teachings of Calvinism hold any ground against this decay since Calvinism itself had grown cold, dogmatic, and intellectual. Clergy failed to give adequate pastoral care to their parishioners. Many new towns received no ministerial support whatsoever. Bishoprics were awarded not on the basis of pastoral ability or spiritual awareness but on the basis of political patronage. Few clergy had any inner zeal for spiritual matters anyway because such "enthusiasm" was frowned upon. By the 1730s the bulk of England's population, particularly the poor, who were not interested in pursuing each new variety of religious thought, were desperate for a religion that affected not only their heads but their hearts. Those abused by poverty, hard work, and increasing vice had emotional needs that Christianity was not meeting.

THE METHODIST MOVEMENT AND THE EVANGELICAL MOVEMENT

Origins of the Two Movements

What changed the religious atmosphere in England was the Evangelical Revival and that began with the conversion of George Whitefield in 1734. His eloquent preaching began to affect great numbers of people in the urban centers years before John Wesley became an itinerant preacher. In fact, it was Whitefield who coaxed Wesley into the open-air ministry. However, Wesley put much more effort into organizing what became the Wesleyan Methodist Church than Whitefield did into organizing the Calvinistic Methodists. Whitefield was far more interested in being an independent evangelist, particularly in being free to conduct his frequent preaching tours in America. Wesley remained in England after his conversion and it was there that his ministry erected the Methodist Movement which would eventually break ties with the Church of England. By the time Wesley died in 1791 it had seventy thousand fully committed members.[34]

The Methodist Movement was a movement among England's poor (though Whitefield had some limited success with the well-to-do he met through the Countess of Huntington.) "Methodism," writes Gerald R. Cragg, "began among poor people; its advance was built upon the pennies they contributed."[35] It was a reaction or a revolt against not only the religion but the society of its day.[36] It provided the people of England with a faith that involved the feelings, not just the intellect, and it emphasized conversion and radically changed lives. It clashed with its culture, scorning the activities that detracted from a person's spiritual-mindedness: cards, theatre, dances, and other amusements. In its ambition to bring back the simplicity and vitality of the New Testament Church many found Methodism austere.[37] Nevertheless, as a religious movement it won a considerable following and exerted a tremendous moral influence, particularly on the young Evangelical Movement.

Wilberforce, for instance, one of the first generation of the Evangelical Movement, was influenced by Methodist teaching in his childhood, and after his conversion in 1785 was counseled by John Newton, devotee of George Whitefield and an Evangelical pastor with Methodist sympathies.[38] Indeed, the line is not always easily drawn between the two groups. There is a great deal of overlap when it comes to Methodism and Evangelicalism and a good deal of common ground is shared by both. Not all scholars make clear distinctions between the two movements and therefore they are unfamiliar with the differences. However, before the Evangelical Movement became a powerful force in British society, the Methodist Movement had already been altering the religious climate in the British Isles for decades.

It has already been noted in Chapter I that there were two evangelical streams in eighteenth century Britain, that of evangelical Dissent, those who did not feel they could in good faith remain within the Church of England, and that of Anglican Evangelicalism, those who felt strongly about remaining loyal to the Church. One of the first Anglican Evangelical pioneers appears to have been William Grimshaw who took up his living as an Evangelical in Howarth in the north of England in 1742.[39] William Romaine began his Evangelical ministry in London in 1749 preaching the Sunday Lectures at St. Dustan's (lectureships had been established under the Stuarts for the purpose of religious education outside of formal worship hours.) In 1764 he was voted rector of St. Andrew-by-the-Wardrobe and for thirteen years he "was the only representative of the [Evangelical] party beneficed north of the Thames."[40] John Newton arrived to take St. Mary Woolnoth in 1779 but the two men remained alone for another twenty years.[41] However, south of the Thames, Evangelical Roger Bentley had taken St. Giles', Camberwell in 1769 and Evangelical William Abdy became curate-in-charge of St. John's, Horsleydown in 1782.[42] Meanwhile, Henry Venn had been the Evangelical curate of Clapham from 1754 until 1759 whereupon he went to Huddersfield, and John Fletcher had begun his Evangelical preaching in Madeley, a large village, in 1760.[43]

The Anglican Evangelical Movement began to coalesce, however, under the leadership of John Thornton, the wealthy London merchant who was half-brother to Wilberforce's aunt, Hannah Wilberforce. It is not only Brown who feels Thornton is the founder of the united Movement. Paul Johnson also believes this to be the case, claiming that the "real founder" of the Evangelical Movement "was John Thornton of Clapham."[44]

John Thornton was converted to Christianity in 1754 by the preaching of George Whitefield.[45] If indeed he can be seen as the father, or a father, of Evangelicalism, his religious influence dates from that year, twenty years after Whitefield's conversion and the advent of the Evangelical Revival. He was zealous for his new-found faith and he did not lack influential contacts in his business with whom he could share his religious beliefs. A peer described him as "very rich, in great credit and esteem, and of as much weight in the City [of London] as any one man I know."[46]

But those whose names came to be synonymous with eighteenth century Evangelicalism were John Newton, William Romaine, Thomas Scott, Charles Simeon, and William Wilberforce, particularly Wilberforce, since "after his [John Thornton's] death in 1790, the leadership devolved on William Wilberforce..."[47] The Evangelical Movement found a larger following among the middle and upper classes, and among the educated—though it did not gain strong support at Oxford, it did at Cambridge.[48] Its impact on society was as far-reaching as that of the Methodist Movement, if not more so.[49] Brown considers that Wesley's ministry laid a foundation "for the work of succeeding reformers with superior methods."[50]

Aspects Held in Common

There is confusion in delineating what was Methodist and what was Evangelical because the two movements were responding to the same spiritual needs of English society and because they had so much in common theologically. Hall and Albion state:

It seemed inevitable to many that there were only two alternatives, the skepticism of Hume and a return to historic Christianity. A large number chose the old trail rather than the new. This, more than any other reason, explains the contemporary evangelical movement within the Church of England, which stressed personal salvation, and likewise the Methodist revival.[51]

Both were Protestant movement, finding common ground in their espousal of Reformation essentials: *sola gratia, sola fide, sola scriptura,* and *solus Christus.* Both emphasized the crucial nature of achieving personal salvation through faith in the atoning sacrifice of Jesus Christ. Both considered that every person was lost in sin and could only be rescued from eternal damnation through this faith in Christ. Both put great weight by the need for a Christian to commune daily with God, to be obedient to God in all daily affairs, and to increase in holiness. In the light of these emphases it is not hard to see why both movements stressed soteriology, evangelism, and personal discipleship.

Both had common links to Pietism and Puritanism. In reaction to the Reformation's emphasis on correct doctrine "Pietism sought a fulfillment of the Reformation in a reformation of life as well as doctrine."[52] Seventeenth-century Puritanism had been concerned with similar objectives, "a reformation or purification in worship as well as in life."[53] Both Pietism and Puritanism "stressed the necessity for the new birth, the experience of the heart, and the reality of regeneration which served as a complement to the Reformation emphasis on justification."[54] It is clear that these emphases became part of Methodism and Evangelicalism. To this heritage Methodism and Evangelicalism added a strong ethical dimension.[55]

Parallels between Puritanism and the two movements are especially obvious. Where the Puritans had filled their pulpits with ministers who constantly preached the gospel, so did the Methodists and Evangelicals. The Puritans had considered High Church adherents nominal Christians, and so did the Methodists and Evangelicals. The Puritans regarded Sunday, the Sabbath, as a holy day, and so did the Methodists and Evangelicals. The Puritans saw many amusements and sports as frivolous and spiritually dangerous—the Methodists and Evangelicals felt the same way. The Puritans placed a great store by the victorious deathbed scenes of Christians and the Methodists and Evangelicals followed suit. The Puritans stressed early rising, spontaneous prayer, Bible and devotional reading, meditation on God, Christ, and Providence—in all this the Methodists and Evangelicals imitated them. With the Puritans, the Methodists and Evangelicals shared a "serious" approach to life and the importance of the emotions and the will, as well as reason and conscience. Methodist and Evangelical leaders like Whitefield and Wesley and Doddridge and Wilberforce steeped themselves in Puritan writings. It is no wonder then that Brown finds the similarities between the Puritans and the Methodists and Evangelicals "striking."[56]

Other than the writings of the Puritans and the Pietists, the single work which had the greatest impact on the development of Methodism and Evangelicalism was William Law's *A Serious Call to a Devout and Holy Life*, published in 1728. It influenced John and Charles Wesley, George Whitefield, Thomas Scott, John Newton, and James Stillingfleet.

> The author recommends the exercise of the moral virtues and meditation and ascetical practices…He insists especially on the virtues practices in everyday life, temperance, humility and self-denial, all animated by the intention to glorify God, to which every human activity should be directed.[57]

For Law, the activities which could be directed to the glory of God were defined: "There are no innocent amusements or relaxations, learning is suspect, and almost everything that comes under the heading of culture is dangerous."[58] His influence on the Evangelicals is clearly evident in Wilberforce's journals and diaries where moderation, humility, and self-denial are constant themes. However, the Evangelicals did not become quite as strict as the Methodists in heeding Law's strictures on amusements, education, and culture.

Differences Between the Two Movements

Though both Wesley and Whitefield remained members of the Church of England, Wesley's structuring of "bands" of Methodist followers in each village and town and city for mutual support, the building of places of worship by both Wesley and Whitefield, the mutual animosity between the Church of England and the Methodists, eventually led to the complete separation of Wesleyan Methodism from Anglicanism. In practical terms, the separation had existed long before the official act. The Evangelical Movement, on the other hand, remained loyal to the Church of England.

During Wilberforce's lifetime the Evangelicals tended to separate themselves less from the general run of society than the Methodists did. A good number of Anglican Evangelicals were generous philanthropists who maintained an upper class lifestyle. In fact, "many of the recognized Evangelical leaders lived in such a style as a matter of deliberate policy,...to make it plain to the upper ranks that Evangelicals were not 'methodistical' but respectable and substantial."[59] It was considered wrong by these Evangelicals to dress beneath one's station. "Piety was not at war with elegance."[60] The Evangelicals were simply not as austere as the Methodists. Even sports such as riding (Charles Simeon), swimming and walking (Thomas Babington), and boating (John Venn) were enjoyed. Nevertheless, all this was to be indulged in, not for its own sake, but so that one might be refreshed for the serious aspects of life.[61]

The Methodists did not encourage Christians to run for public office, stressing a separation from "worldy" society and political affairs. The first generation of Evangelicals did just the opposite, feeling called to serve Christ in all manner of public life. And where the Methodists did not put a great store by higher education, many of the Evangelicals of Wilberforce's day certainly did. "Faith," states Rosman, "often provided an incentive for study which many evangelicals thoroughly enjoyed."[62]

John Wesley's influence was not strong among Evangelicals, as it was among the Wesleyan Methodists. Some Evangelicals, like John Newton and Thomas Scott, held to Calvinistic principles. They spoke in terms of limited atonement and of predestination rather than the more Arminian ideas of an unlimited atonement and the free will of humans espoused by Wesley. Nor did Evangelicals share Wesley's belief in the possibility of the perfection of the human soul before death. However, it must be cautioned that many Evangelicals, including Wilberforce, were not thorough-going Calvinists, and that the two movements shared far more doctrinally than they differed. The greatest gap between the two movements, therefore, appears to be in their disparate approaches to culture. The Methodists were more at odds with English culture than the Evangelicals were. Thus, Ian Bradley, W.R. Ward, Haddon Wilmer, and Doreen M. Rosman argue that Evangelicalism was not the reaction to English society that Methodism was, but in fact was a product of that society and manifested many of its traits.[63] It became more widely accepted than Methodism, thus causing a moral and spiritual reformation of greater proportions, because its principles were, to a reasonable extent, suitable to the social milieu from which Evangelicalism sprang, and in which it was relatively comfortable.[64]

Notes

1. Brown, p. 4.

2. Ibid., P. 5.

3. Ibid., p. 4.

4. Ervine, p. 213.

5. Wilberforce, quoted in *William Jay, The Autobiography of William Jay,* ed. George Redford and John Angell James (1854; reprint ed., Edinburgh: The Banner of Truth Trust, 1974), p. 309.

6. Richard A. Alcock, *World Literature* (New York: Greystone Press, 1957), p. 36.

7. Ervine, p. 248.

8. See Walter Phelps Hall and Robert G. Albion, *A History of England and the British Empire* (London: Ginn & Co., 1937), p. 488; Keith Feiling, *A History of England* (London: Macmillan, 1950), p. 686.

9. Brown, p. 21.

10. Ibid.

11. Ibid., p. 24

12. Ibid., p. 25.

13. Wilberforce, Hull MS Diary, 3 Feb. 1818, quoted in John Pollock, *Wilberforce* (London: Constable, 1977), p. 263. See also pp. 59, 262.

14. Feiling, p. 684.

15. Oliver Warner, *William Wilberforce* (London: B.T. Batsford Ltd., 1962), p. 18.

16. Ibid., p. 19.

17. Ibid.

18. Ibid., p. 20.

19. Hall and Albion, p. 505.

20. See Robin Furneaux, *William Wilberforce* (London: Hamish Hamilton, 1974), p. 177; Garth Lean, *God's Politician* (London: Darton, Longman and Todd, 1980), p. 152.

21. Jack C. Estrin, *World History* (New York: Greystone Press, 1957), p. 162.

22. Ibid.

23. See Pollock, pp. 142, 256, 263; Coupland, pp. 359-60; Brown, pp. 246, 341.

24. Lean, p. 102.

25. Pollock, p. 180.

26. Alcock, p. 94.

27. Ibid., pp. 94-5.

28. Ibid., p. 95.

29. Hall and Albion, p. 519.

30. Alcock, p. 95.

31. Feiling, p. 695.

32. Alcock, p. 94.

33. Brown, p. 37.

34. Feiling, p. 698.

35. Gerald R. Cragg, *The Church and the Age of Reason* (Markham: Pengiun, 1960), p. 149.

36. See Hall and Albion, p. 524; Cragg, p. 153.

37. Hall and Albion, p. 525.

38. Lean, p. 35.

39. Balleine, pp. 46-7.

40. Ibid., pp. 43-4.

41. Ibid., p. 44.

42. Ibid.

43. Ibid., pp. 40, 51, 59.

44. Paul Johnson, *A History of Christianity* (1976; reprint ed., Markham: Pelican, 1980), p. 369; Brown, p. 78.

45. Pollock, p. 5.

46. Ibid.

47. Johnson, p. 370.

48. Cragg, pp. 152-4.

49. Brown, p. 4.

50. Ibid.

51. Hall and Albion, p. 524.

52. Bloesch, 1:11. German Pietism influenced the Methodist Movement, and consequently the Evangelical Movement, after John Wesley came in contact with, and was initially impressed by, Peter Bohler and the Moravian Brethren. See *The Westminster Dictionary of Christian Spirituality*, 1983 ed., s.v. "Moravian Spirituality," by Gordon S. Wakefield.

53. Bloesch, 1:11.

54. Ibid.

55. Ibid.

56. Brown, p. 169.

57. *Oxford Dictionary of the Christian Church*, cited by *WDCS*, 1983 ed., s.v. "Nonjurors," by W. Jardine Grisbrooke.

58. *WDCS*, ibid.

59. Brown, p. 58.

60. Hannah More, *Strictures on the Modern System of Female Education,* vol. 3 of *Works* (London, 1834), p. 60, cited by Rosman, p. 87.

61. Ibid., p. 121.

62. Ibid., p. 223.

63. Ibid., pp. 7-9.

64. Ian Bradley, *The Call to Seriousness* (New York: Macmillan, 1976); W.R. Ward, *Religion and Society in England,* 1790-1850 (London, 1972); Haddon Willmer, "Evangelicalism, 1785-1830" (Husean prize Essay, Cambridge University, 1962).

CHAPTER III

Wilberforce's Spiritual Formation

His development from birth to death

William Wilberforce was born in Hull in 1759, where his spiritual journey began in an Anglican household: "I was born of parents religious according to the old school."[1] Though his mother did not yet hold "those views of the spiritual nature of religion which she adopted later in life,"[2] enough of the faith of the Church of England was worked into him to keep him attached to it for the rest of his life. Baptized as an infant, he never broke from the Anglican Church and, particularly after his conversion to an Evangelical faith, he enjoyed worship in the Established Church, finding great benefit in both the liturgy and the sacrament of Holy Eucharist.[3]

The Young Methodist (1769-70)

Progress in Wilberforce's religious development took place when he was nine. His father died and Wilberforce was sent to live with an uncle and aunt, William and Hannah Wilberforce, at Wimbledon and St. James' Place. They took him to hear Evangelical sermons at the parish church in nearby Clapham, for the aunt was a strong admirer of George Whitefield, the leader of Calvinistic Methodism who died on a preaching tour of the American colonies in 1770. At Clapham, Wilberforce heard another admirer of George Whitefield preach—John Newton, the converted slave trader. His influence on the young Wilberforce was great: "I reverenced him as a parent when I was a child."[4]

It was not just Newton and his preaching which influenced him. Even Wilberforce's High Church sons had to admit the positive effects of his aunt and uncle's strongly religious life on the young Anglican: "There can be little doubt that the acquaintance with holy Scripture and the habits of devotion which he then acquired, fostered that baptismal seed which though long dormant was destined to produce at last a golden harvest."[5] Wilberforce himself later wrote of this period:

> Under these influences my mind was interested by religious subjects. How far these impressions were genuine I can hardly determine, but at least I many venture to say that I was sincere. There are letters of mine, written at that period, still in existence, which accord much with my present sentiments.[6]

A third influence on his religious development during these years was John Thornton, his aunt's half-brother and the man Brown and Johnson consider the founder of the Evangelical Movement. He often visited Hannah and William Wilberforce and took an interest in their nephew. On one occasion Thornton gave Wilberforce a sum of cash as a gift, but it was given with the understanding that he learn to part with some of the money in the form of aid for the poor.[7]

By the time Wilberforce was twelve he had developed, writes Robin Furneaux, into "a devout and surprisingly mature Methodist."[8] His mother would have none of it. As Wilberforce's letters became increasingly Evangelical, she arrived to take the boy home to Hull. The religious enthusiasm of Methodism was abhorrent to most Anglicans and Wilberforce's mother was no exception. There was a painful scene as he was taken from his aunt and uncle. They felt that he was being deprived of a religious life. But though there would be a lapse in Wilberforce's spiritual odyssey, the roots formed at Wimbledon would prove tenacious enough to grow back and become a part of his adult spirituality thirteen years later.

Was the time spent at Wimbledon the occasion of something like a first conversion? Furneaux thinks so:

> He underwent two conversions; the first took place when as a boy he stayed with a Methodist uncle in Wimbledon...On learning the news his mother descended, removed Wilberforce and set about the undermining of his faith...Eleven years later, in 1785, he experienced a second and permanent conversion.[9]

Certainly a powerful religious impression had been stamped on his personality. "One at least who then met him," write his sons, "remarked in him a rare and pleasing character of piety in his twelfth year."[10] The task of rooting out this new-found faith was not easy.

The Years Before Conversion (1771-84)

For three years Wilberforce corresponded with his uncle and aunt, wrestling to keep his faith alive. At the age of thirteen he wrote to his aunt:

> One of the greatest misfortunes I had whilst at Hull was, not being able to hear the blessed word of God, as my mama would not let me go to high church on a Sunday afternoon; but the Lord was everyday granting me some petition, and I trust I can say that I increased in the knowledge of God and Christ whom he sent, whom to know is life eternal.[11]

Two years before his death Wilberforce complained that these letters were "rather too much in the style of the religious letters of that day."[12] Yet, he admitted, "I cannot doubt my having expressed sentiments and feelings of my heart."[13] But these "sentiments" were eventually submerged under the weight of Hull's social life: the theatre, the balls, the great suppers, the card parties. "The religious impressions which I had gained at Wimbledon continued for a considerable time after my return to Hull," he said, "but my friends spared no pains to stifle them."[14] The last religious letter to his aunt was written on May 19, 1774, when Wilberforce was fifteen.[15] However, he later reminisced concerning this demise of his young faith:

How visibly...I can trace the hand of God leading me by ways which I knew not!...My mother's taking me from my uncle's when about twelve or thirteen and then completely a Methodist, has probably been the means of my being connected with political men and becoming useful in life. If I had staid with my uncle I should probably have been a bigoted despised methodist.[16]

When he became MP for Hull in 1780, Wilberforce began to attend Anglican services in London.[17] Sometimes Pitt joined him.[18] If mainstream Anglicanism can indeed be said to be the religion of the gentleman,[19] then Wilberforce's religious thinking by this time had become more of the gentleman's and less of the enthusiast's. During a trip to the Lake District in 1779 he had written:

Went in the morning to the Vicarage Garden. The view sweetly pastoral and the church though new a fine object. It rises as venerable as is consistent with simplicity and humility.[20]

Nevertheless, despite the fact that his Methodist fires had cooled almost to extinction, Wilberforce was considered a religious man by his friends and peers.[21] His morals and principles were high. He attributed this religious spirit to his relish for the solitude of the country. On June 5, 1783, when he was twenty-three years old, he wrote his sister a letter from Wimbledon:

If my moral and religious principles be such as in these days are not very generally prevalent, perhaps I owe the continuance of them in a great measure to solitude in the country...in the country a little reading or reflection...and we become sensible of our own imperfections.[22]

His love for the country, for solitude, for religious reading, for reflection, his habit of examining himself for imperfections, the importance of humility, all these would stay on to become permanent traits of his Evangelical spirituality in the years ahead. At this point, they were probably a result of a combination of factors: his renewed Anglicanism with its emphasis on the moralistic, the principled, and the reasonable; the habits ingrained in him at Wimbledon which he unconsciously acted out in terms of his new religious interests; his awakening appreciation for certain aspects of Unitarian teaching with its emphasis on reason, conscience, and character.

The services of the Church of England which Wilberforce attended in Wimbledon and London would have reflected the spirit of the age which was discussed in Chapter II. Gerald R. Cragg comments:

> Churchmanship…was not inspiring…In outlook it was neither mystical nor otherworldly. It set exaggerated store by moderation, and the qualities it esteemed most highly were temperance, restraint, and reasonableness. It had little sympathy with the more austere virtues and studiously ignored the claims of self-denial. It adapted itself all too readily to the tastes of an age which exalted common sense and pursued material prosperity…Even in its worthiest representative it lacked originality, poetic sensibility, and prophetic insight;…[23]

Yet the Anglican Church had its strong points too. Morality was emphasized over and against the licentiousness of the age and most sermons had an ethical rather than a dogmatic tone that would have appealed to Wilberforce.[24] An apologetic was developed that was vigorous, extensive, and based on sound scholarship.[25] Nevertheless, it remains that the Church had eliminated the need for salvation by faith by substituting moralism in its stead and worship had become emotionally dry and "pedestrian."[26] Despite the benefits Wilberforce had accrued from his Anglican faith, he still sensed a certain lack which manifested itself in his interest in some of the teachings of Theophilus Lindsey.

Lindsey was a former Anglican clergyman who had resigned his living when he stopped believing in the deity of Christ. Breaking ties with the Church of England he had founded his own chapel on Essex Street where Wilberforce had a sitting.[27] A man who espoused what were then called Socinian ideas—named for Faustus and Laelius Socinus, Italian Protestant theologians of the sixteenth century who rejected many key Christian doctrines—Lindsey has become known as the father of modern Unitarianism.[28] Lindsey and his followers worshipped God, but, in line with Faustus and Laelius Socinus, denied the deity of Christ, the Trinity, the authority of Scripture, and the Christian view of the Atonement (though Lindsey continued to preach the Christian ethic and to read the Anglican service.)[29] By the time of his re-election as MP for York in April of 1784, Wilberforce at twenty-four considered Lindsey London's only zealous preacher.[30] He did not attend Lindsey's chapel because of the man's Socinian/Unitarian ideas, he remained too much of an Anglican for that. He went to listen to him because Lindsey preached an easily applied practical religion. "He seemed," said Wilberforce, "more earnest and practical than others."[31] This passion for practical religion would also be a hallmark of his Evangelical spirituality.

Wilberforce began his gradual conversion to an Evangelical Christianity in 1784 when he embarked on a tour of continental Europe with members of his family and a traveling companion named Isaac Milner. On only two occasions prior to this trip did Wilberforce actually come into close contact with Evangelicalism. The first was when he heard Charles Edward De Coetlogon preach at Lock Chapel on December 7, 1783.[32] The chapel, connected with a hospital and asylum for women suffering with venereal disease, was both Anglican and Evangelical and it is unlikely that Wilberforce did not know this before he attended.[33] He certainly knew of De Coetlogon's reputation and this is another example of Wilberforce searching beyond a High Church setting for something more than he was being offered there. De Coetlogon had both his BA and his MA from Pembroke College, Cambridge, and after being ordained was appointed assistant chaplain at Lock Chapel where he swiftly gained popularity for his eloquent and Calvinistic preaching.[34]

The second contact with Evangelicalism was a meal with Sir Charles Middleton in the same month.[35] A Navy man and an Evangelical, he had stopped cursing and blasphemy on his ships, nor did he allow any work in the Portsmouth Navy Yard on Sunday. There is no indication from Wilberforce's papers as to the effect, if any, these pre-conversion brushes with the Evangelical faith had on him.

The Great Change (1785)

In the fall of the year in which Wilberforce was elected MP for York, he invited the Rev. Isaac Newton to accompany him on a continental tour. The two men had spent some time with each other that summer in Scarborough and Wilberforce had enjoyed Milner's energetic conversation.[36] Milner had been Wilberforce's usher at the Hull Grammar School in 1767 when Wilberforce was eight but the two had met only briefly at that time.[37] Now Milner was a clergyman and a tutor at Queen's College, Cambridge, which Wilberforce knew, and an Evangelical, which Wilberforce did not know. Milner accepted the invitation and the party set out in October of 1784. There were two carriages, one with Wilberforce and Milner, another with Wilberforce's mother and sister and two female relatives. The two men began to argue at the beginning of the journey when they were still in England. Wilberforce criticized James Stillingfleet, the Evangelical rector of Hotham, calling him a good man who took things too far. "No," Milner responded. "How does he take things too far?"[38] Milner's response surprised Wilberforce. He later wrote that if he had known Milner was an Evangelical "it would have decided me against making him the offer" of accompanying him to France.[39]

The two debated religion all the way to the French Riviera but Milner's case for an Evangelical faith made little impact on Wilberforce. As they were about to leave the women at the Riviera and return to England at the beginning of 1785, Wilberforce "took up casually a little volume" belonging to one of his female cousins.[40] It was Philip Doddridge's *The Rise and Progress of Religion in the Soul.* "It is one of the best books ever written," Milner told Wilberforce. "Let us take it with us and read it on our journey."[41] Their study and discussion of the book had such an effect on Wilberforce "that he determined at some future season to examine the Scriptures for himself, and see if things were stated there in the same manner."[42] Therefore, as soon as Parliament recessed for the summer, Wilberforce and Milner returned by coach to the continent and met the ladies at Genoa.[43] Journeying on to Switzerland, the men examined the Greek New Testament and its doctrines: Wilberforce had learned Greek as an undergraduate at Cambridge where he had studied from 1776 to 1779.[44] Milner, who had a gift for teaching, now began to make some headway with Wilberforce. "I got," said Wilberforce many years later, "a clear idea of the doctrines of Religion perhaps clearer than I have had since, but it was quite in my head."[45] But, he confessed, "by degrees I imbibed his [Milner's] sentiments."[46]

The party spent nearly six weeks at the Belgian resort of Spa. Here, though enjoying himself, Wilberforce shied away from attending plays and from traveling on Sundays. He began to battle inwardly a fear of damnation.[47]

> I had received into my understanding the great truths of the gospel, and believed that its offers were free and universal; and that God had promised to give his Holy Spirit to them that asked for it. At length such thoughts as these completely occupied my mind, and I began to pray earnestly.[48]

By October 21 or 22 he began to get up early to pray in the quiet hours of the morning.[49] He had an overwhelming sense of guilt and condemnation which remained with him on his return to England in November. His dread of damnation was overshadowed by his realization that for years he had neglected God and Christ. "Such was the effect," he wrote, "which this thought produced, that for months I was in a state of the deepest depression, from strong convictions of my guilt. Indeed nothing which I have ever read in the accounts of others exceeded what I then felt."[50]

He began a journal to make himself "humble and watchful."[51] He began to read the Bible or have it read to him. He read Blaise Pascal. He read Bishop Butler.[52] He got up at six in the morning for thirty minutes of private devotions. He spent time meditating. He initiated family prayer in the mornings and evenings. He prayed fervently by himself. Finally, at the close of the month of November, he thought of going to see John Newton, his "boyhood hero,"[53] as John Pollock puts it. He counted on getting help from the minister's prayers and experience.[54]

Newton was now sixty and rector of St. Mary Woolnoth in London. After vacillation, Wilberforce wrote to Newton on December 2, spurred perhaps by the Evangelical sermon he had heard Henry Foster of Long Acre Chapel give that day in his lecture at St. Antholyn's—"If you seek him, he will be found by you, but if you forsake him, he will forsake you."[55] However, he did not send the note. On December 3 he saw Pitt, to whom he had written about his religious experience. Pitt did not ridicule but respected his friend's conversion, though he tried unsuccessfully to talk him out of it. On December 4 Wilberforce had his note to Newton delivered, making an appointment to see him December 7. He honored the commitment with some trepidation, afraid the meeting with Newton might become public knowledge. Garth Lean comments,

> It was perhaps natural that the successful politician should find it hard to approach the man who typified the faith and affection he had known as a boy and then rejected to the point of ridicule. But the key reason for his hesitation was...an unwillingness to identify himself with the most militant Christianity of the day.[56]

But Wilberforce found comfort in Newton's counsel:

> He told me he always had entertained hopes and confidence that God would some time bring me to Him...When I came away I found my mind in a calm, tranquil state, more humbled, and looking more devoutly up to God.[57]

On June 27, 1795, Wilberforce wrote a letter to Mr. O'Hara regarding the period of time between the demise of his youthful Methodism and his adult conversion to Evangelical Christianity. "I seem," he observed, "to have awakened about nine or ten years ago from a dream, to have recovered, as it were, the use of my reason after a delirium."[58] By the beginning of 1786 this conversion, "or perhaps Re-dedication to the Christ of his boyhood faith," as Pollock suggests,[59] was solidly established in Wilberforce's being. He no longer cringed from identification with the faith he had shunned for ten years. On January 12, 1786, while Wilberforce and Newton were walking together in the evening, an acquaintance of Wilberforce stumbled upon them unexpectedly. Wilberforce wrote stalwartly in his diary: "Expect to hear myself now universally given out to be a Methodist: may God grant it may be said with truth."[60]

Early Struggles as a Christian (1786-7)

If, as Michael Hennell suggests, "the main ingredients of evangelical spirituality have always been early rising, prayer and Bible study,"[61] Wilberforce was well on his way as a convert to the Evangelical faith. On October 25, 1785 at Spa, he had written: "Began three or four days ago to get up very early. In the solitude and self-conversation of the morning had thoughts which I trust will come to something."[62] From this point he developed a pattern of early morning prayer, meditation, and Bible study which lasted the rest of his life. Where did he get the idea to commence this life-long practice?

Did Milner encourage it? There is no evidence that he did. Did Newton coax it along? It seems likely that he would have for Wilberforce relied on Newton's advice a great deal during this period, but there is no clear evidence that Newton guided him in this area. However, Doddridge speaks of this pattern of religious disciplines at some length in *The Rise and Progress of Religion in the Soul* which Wilberforce had read. Doddridge passed these disciplines along from his readings in the Puritans.[63] He advised:

In the beginning of the day, it should certainly be our care, —to lift up our hearts to God as soon as we wake,…and then, to set ourselves immediately to the secret devotions of the morning…To begin the stated devotions of the day with the solemn act of praise,…After this, to take a prospect of the day before us, so far as we can see in the general, where and how it may be spent; and seriously to reflect, How shall I employ myself for God this day?…What temptations am I likely to be assaulted with…? In what instances have I lately failed?…After this review, it would be proper to offer up a short prayer,… I would advise you after this, to read some portion of Scripture;…considering them merely in a devotional and practical view.[64]

Nor it is unreasonable to surmise that habits learned from his Methodist uncle and aunt fifteen years before reasserted themselves as a means with which to commune with God and self during a difficult and confused phase in Wilberforce's life—his faith as a man was constantly touched by his faith when a boy. Finally, he was already noted as a man who loved solitude, reflection, and inspirational reading. The cumulative effect was for Wilberforce to take his relationship with God and the consequent necessity of his spiritual development very seriously.

He struggled to discipline himself. Personal rules concerning the management of his time were established, broken and re-established.[65] Whenever he was lax in his personal devotions he came down hard on himself. He berated himself so frequently the pages of his journals and diaries often seem oppressive to the reader:

> I see plainly that I am an ungrateful, stupid, guilty creature.[66]

> That wandering spirit and indolent way of doing business are little if at all defeated, and my rules, resolved on with thought and prayer, are forgotten.[67]

> I say solemnly in the presence of God this day, that were I to die, I know not what would be my eternal portion...[68]

> The sense of God's presence seldom stays on my mind when I am in company; and at times I even have doubts and difficulties about the truth of the great doctrines of Christianity.[69]

He recorded the week's "chief temptations" so that he could avoid them.[70] To stop his mind from wandering during prayer, he put his prayers into words.[71] He determined to make his conversation the kind that would open people up to Christian principles.[72] Yet, with all his rules he remembered to trust his spiritual development more to Christ and less to his own resolve.[73] All of this "spiritual temperature-taking" was another Puritan influence mediated through Doddridge's book.[74]

Wilberforce pushed himself hard from the very beginning and he never relented. This was because he had grasped early that his relationship with God was the crux of his faith—if he lost communion with God, he lost everything. "How does my experience convince me," he wrote, "that true religion is to maintain communion with God, and that it all goes together."[75] In the spring of 1786 he said that he had devoted himself "for whatever might be the term of my future life, to the service of my God and Saviour,"[76] and he realized that in order to be "useful" to God he had to remain close to Christ, so that he had to discipline his mind and his body.

It is easy to make the same mistake in reading Wilberforce's journals and the diaries that others have made in reading the private papers of the Puritans, and that is to perceive the dark self-scrutiny found there in an exclusive sense, as somehow indicative of the whole of the man. But the keeping of a personal journal, a habit the Methodists and Evangelicals inherited from the Puritans of the sixteenth and seventeenth centuries, was meant to be a place to talk especially about one's sins in order to be able to see them better and in so doing be able to overcome them. William Haller states:

> It was of the very essence of Puritan self-discipline that whatso-ever thoughts and actions the old Adam within had most desire to keep hidden, the very worst abominations of the heart, one must when one retired to one's chamber at night draw forth into the light of conscience…[77]

Journal keeping actually began within the Christian tradition with some of the writings of Augustine, notably the *Confessions*. Augustine, says Francis Dorff, was "prompted to write down his innermost thoughts and discoveries so that he might become still more animated in his search for truth."[78] This form of writing carried on into the monastic tradition with some of the writings of Bernard of Clairvaux, William of Saint-Thierry, and Bonaventure who used journaling in their attempts to internalize Scripture.[79] The use of a journal was picked up by the Reformers. Dorff states:

> Within the Reformation tradition, the emphasis on personal religious experience gives journal writing a place of special

prominence as a spiritual discipline. The journals of the Pilgrims and Quakers…give eloquent witness to this renewal…[80]

It was John Wesley who brought journaling into Methodism. R.W. Gribben notes the important influence of Wesley's mother Susanna and his Puritan forebears in the formation of his religious habits, including journal writing.[81] Adam Clarke, one of Wesley's preachers and later an important Methodist theologian, said Wesley learned to keep a diary or a journal from his Puritan grandfather John Wesley.[82] The founder of Methodism was also encouraged by his father Samuel to imitate his grandfather in this practice.[83] Bishop Jeremy Taylor, as Wesley mentions in the introduction to his *Journal*, only inspired Wesley to be more precise in his journal keeping.[84] The habit had already been formed early on. His brother Charles also kept a journal and so did George Whitefield (both had been members of the 'Holy Club' at Oxford along with John). John Wesley passed the practice on in the *Large Minutes*, a pamphlet which summed up the rules and practices of Methodism.[85] It was inevitable that the Evangelicals, influenced as they were by both the Puritans and the Methodists, should include journaling as part of their spiritual pedigree. Hennell comments:

> Evangelicals kept a diary, not as a means of recording events, but of self-examination of the recent past and adjustment to the future; it was the evangelical equivalent of the confessional.[86]

The journal was meant to spur one on, to keep one's attention fixed on the goal of godliness or holiness. These were the reasons Wilberforce used it. To suggest from his journal that he was a gloomy, morbid, and humorless individual who slunk the corridors of the House of Commons spreading depression and guilt could not be further from the truth. As Pollock complains,

> In printing them [entries in Wilberforce's journals and diaries] by the yard five years after his death his sons gave the public a view of their father which lacked perspective, for none of the playfulness of his letter writing obtruded into the diary, nor the exuberance and joyousness which delighted his friends.[87]

Wilberforce was a man with an optimistic temperament, an individual whose company was relished by all sorts of people because of his charm, wit, and good humor. His religious faith, as Lean points out, did not detract from these personal gifts, but enhanced them:

> By mid-1786…he had recovered much of the gaiety which delighted his friends….His mother, who had been thoroughly alarmed by reports of his return to 'Methodism', was pleasantly surprised by his cheerfulness and the disappearance of his quick temper. 'If this is madness,' said her friend, Mrs. Sykes, 'I hope he will bite us all.'[88]

In spite of Wilberforce's struggles at self-control, John Wesley's proverb, "Sour godliness is the Devil's religion," could never be applied to the young convert. "Interior severity," notes Pollock, "helped create the joy which he considered a mark of genuine Christianity."[89] Years later Wilberforce would write a friend about the centrality of joy in the Christian's life, a joy which, if barely hinted at in the sin-exposing atmosphere of the journal-confessional, marked all his days an Evangelical believer:

> My grand objection to the religious system still held by many who declare themselves orthodox Churchmen…is, that it tends to render Christianity so much a system of prohibitions rather than of privilege and hopes, and thus the injunction to rejoice so strongly enforced in the New Testament is practically neglected, and Religion is made to wear a forbidding and gloomy air and not one of peace and hope and joy.[90]

A Dark Night of the Soul (1788)

On the eve of launching one of the most important causes of his political career, the battle for Abolition, Wilberforce almost lost his life. He had never had a strong physical constitution, suffering from weak eyes and an intestinal disorder that was probably ulcerative colitis.[91] Now this disorder began to work on him. Wilberforce lost his appetite, ran a fever, was plagued by thirst, became insomniac. He would recover for a day or two only to relapse again. He became progressively weaker until in late March his physicians declared that "he had not the stamina to last a fortnight."[92] It was the placing of Wilberforce on a lifelong course of opium which saved his life. Once the opium reversed Wilberforce's near-fatal condition, it only remained for him to spend some time at the waters of Bath in order to recover completely.

At death's door, Wilberforce had apparently kept a small red leather notebook entitled "March, 1788."[93] The notebook records his spiritual struggles during this time, making use of prayers from *The Book of Common Prayer* and other volumes, and including many of his informal prayers. In the first of the latter of these he cries:

> Lord, thou knowest that no strength, wisdom or contrivance of human power can signify, or relieve me. It is in thy power alone to deliver me. I fly to thee for succour and support, O Lord let it come speedily; give me full proof of thy Almighty power; I am in great troubles, unsurmountable by me; but to thee slight and inconsiderable; look upon me O Lord with compassion and mercy, and restore me to rest, quietness, and comfort, in the world, or in another by removing me hence into a state of peace and happiness. Amen.[94]

A second prayer suggests that he was being treated with opium and had some hope for a recovery, for he was looking ahead and contemplating an embattled future, probably due to the cause of Abolition which he anticipated leading when he became fully well.[95] At one point a terrible prayer seems to indicate that the delusional and depressive side-effects of opium were assaulting him: "Corrupt imaginations are perpetually rising in my mind and innumerable fears close me in on every side…"[96] Finally, the worst is over. Pollock, who has had access to the notebook, comments,

> By the time he stops using the notebook his prayers ask calmly for grace to do his duty, freedom from worldly motives, from desire for applause and from the temptation to depend on human aid alone.[97]

Indeed, if Wilberforce needed any more motivation towards

improving his relationship with God, his scrape with death certainly provided it. At a summer residence in the Lake District he returned with vigor to his personal rules:

> I will now form and note in my pocket-book such resolutions for this week's regulation, as are best adapted to my present circumstances; and do thou, O God, enable me to keep them. My general object, during my stay at this place, should be to guard against habits of idleness, luxury, selfishness, and forgetfulness of God, by interlacing as much as I can of reading, meditation, and religious retirement, and self-examination.[98]

Constantly mindful of disciplining himself so that he might serve God better in his career, he adds, "Let me constantly view myself in all my various relations as one who professes to be a Christian, as a member of parliament, as gifted by nature and fortune, as a son, brother, paterfamilias, friend, with influence and powerful connections."[99] His dark night of the soul was over. He was ready to return to the House of Commons and serve Christ in his important seat as one of the MPs for Yorkshire.

The Years of Commitment (1789-1824)

For the next thirty-six years Wilberforce would be at the peak of his powers as he fought the British and European slave trades and took on a host of other projects, including the emancipation of the slaves themselves. It was crucial to him that God not be neglected because of a busy schedule. His devotional times not only refreshed him spiritually but composed him so that he was more efficient in his business matters. Coupland considered Wilberforce's devotions to be the source of his endurance in his political struggles: "There lies the secret of Wilberforce's indomitable perseverance. These religious devotions would seem, indeed, to have become an almost indispensable tonic for his mercurial temperament. They steadied, refreshed, inspired him..."[100]

Wilberforce began keeping carefully organized schedules in early 1789 in order to manage his time more wisely. They showed how his time was actually spent: so much in study, so much in necessary visits, so much in dressing, in eating, in relaxation, in bed, in "serious" reading and meditation. They also showed how much time was "squandered." When Parliament was sitting anywhere from three to eleven hours might be spent in the House of Commons, but his time for reading, meditation, and prayer was never less than thirty minutes, generally forty-five minutes to an hour.[101] (On a particularly busy day, January 27, 1789, he spent eleven hours in the House, but prepared for it by spending a solid hour on his private devotions).[102] On holidays he spent considerable time in study (with a view to developing himself intellectually), a good amount of time in relaxation (something he rarely did when Parliament was in session), and usually an hour for devotions. On religious holidays such as Good Friday and Easter Sunday, he spent between four and five hours or more in prayer and Scripture reading.[103]

Wilberforce packed a great deal of devotional activity into his daily routine. "For the ensuing week I resolve to begin the day with meditation or reading Scripture—to pray thrice—constant self-examination—table rules—Horneck's rules—and my other rules—an account of time also."[104] "Prayer three times a day at least and begin with serious reading or contemplation."[105] At week's end, Sunday was crucial for him (and other Evangelicals). He would regularly take the sacrament of Eucharist at an Anglican church and spend the greater portion of the day in communion with God. "Blessed be God who hath appointed these solemn returns of the day of rest to remind us of these most important realities, of which we grow forgetful amidst the hurry of business and the vanities of the world."[106] He would sit under the preaching of Evangelicals like Thomas Scott, Henry Foster, Richard Cecil, William Romaine, and, of course, John Newton.[107] Eleven years before his death he remarked in a letter,

> I am persuaded that to withdraw the mind one day in seven from its ordinary trains of thought and passion, and to occupy it in contemplating subjects of a higher order, which by their magnitude make worldly interests shrink into littleness, has the happiest effect on the intellectual and moral system. It gives us

back on the Monday to the contemplation of our week-day business cooled and quieted, and it is to be hoped with resentments abated, and prejudices softened.[108]

Sunday had been extremely important to the Puritans and they had striven to see it kept as a day of holiness and a time of rest from the week's labors. The example inspired Wilberforce and the Evangelicals. Hennell notes:

Sunday observance was considered an essential part of evangelical spirituality. On Sunday afternoons Wilberforce, carrying Baxter's Works or some other spiritual classic, would leave his guests to themselves.[109]

Sunday was so important to Wilberforce that he felt it must become important for all England as well. Accordingly, he and Lord Belgrave promoted a Bill to suppress Sunday newspapers (which failed). He also helped found the Society for the Better Observance of Sunday in 1800. When Spencer Perceval, an Evangelical, became Prime Minister in 1809 Wilberforce persuaded him to assemble Parliament on Tuesdays instead of Mondays in order to preserve MPs from the sin of traveling on the Sabbath.[110] Wilberforce considered that the keeping of the "Lord's Day" was the factor "on which the very existence of religion" depended in England.[111] Nevertheless, Wilberforce stressed a moderate Sunday observance rather than a rigid one. In 1821 he wrote in a letter:

Often good people have been led by the terms of the Fourth Commandment to lay more stress on the strictness of the Sunday than on its spirituality.[112]

His Sundays in solitude were augmented by excursions away from urban life into some isolated part of the country. Wilberforce had always loved the country and now it became for him a window to God. In a letter to Lord Muncaster in 1804 he said:

I am staying to-day in the country, enjoying the first greetings of summer—the nightingales are abundant, and, my dear friend, while through nature I look up to nature's God, and still more when, from regarding the Author of nature, I further contemplate Him in the still more endearing character of the God of all grace and consolation, my heart is warmed and thankful for the unequalled blessings I enjoy.[113]

He deemed these excursions critical to his spiritual and emotional health: "I wish I could sentence some of my friends to a little solitary imprisonment. They might then see things in their true dimensions."[114]

He also had special days in the year set apart for prayer and self-examination. He not only brought to mind and confessed present sins but also ones he had committed years before, in order to humble himself and direct his thoughts to God's love and salvation.[115] Despite his weak constitution, he fasted, and he helped organize a national fast day in 1803.[116] Birthdays, the New Year, anniversaries of various occasions (such as his conversion or a providential escape from death)—all these furnished opportunities for measuring his spiritual progress, giving thanks to God, prayer, meditation, and confession. Thus in August of 1789 he wrote, "To-morrow I complete my thirtieth year. What shame ought to cover me when I review my past life in all its circumstances!"[117] In 1811, when he turned fifty-two, he recorded the following:

Surely when I look over in detail for the last forty years...when I sum up all together,...I am lost in astonishment, and can only exclaim 'Thy ways are not as our ways, nor Thy thoughts as our thoughts.' I will try to look back through my past life, and to affect my heart, as by review it ought to be, with humiliation, gratitude, love, and confidence, mixed with reverential fear.[118]

New Year's was a time for the Eucharist, a review of his past, and for devoting the coming year to God.[119] An escape from drowning in 1803 was recalled throughout his life, such as in 1818: "To-morrow...is the anniversary of the day in which I experienced that notable escape from being drowned in the Avon...Praise the Lord, O my soul."[120]

Family prayer was also a crucial element in Wilberforce's spirituality as indeed it was for all Evangelicals. Hennell states:

> Family prayers were expected to take part in every evangelical household, the head of the household calling his family and servants together every morning and evening and reading a portion of scripture before the prayers.[121]

Wilberforce followed these guidelines. After he was married in 1797 and he and his wife Barbara began to raise a family, family devotions were included in Wilberforce's daily schedule. They occurred twice a day, Wilberforce expounding briefly each time on a passage of Scripture which was then followed by ten minutes of extempore prayer by family members and servants. Wilberforce encouraged these prayers to be cheerful. What family prayers were like at the Wilberforce home has been preserved by Marianne Thornton. She was Henry Thornton's eldest child (Henry Thornton was Wilberforce's cousin and a member of the Clapham Group). She recorded the following account:

> The scene at prayers is a most curious one. There is a bell which rings when Mr. Wilberforce begins to dress; another when he finishes dressing; upon which Mr. Barningham begins to play a hymn upon the organ and sing a solo, and by degrees the family come down to the entrance hall where the psalmody goes on; first one joins in and then another;... [Wilberforce is] waving his arms about and occasionally pulling the leaves off the geraniums and smelling them, singing out louder and louder in a tone of hilarity. Trust Him, praise Him, trust him, praise Him evermore.[122]

All these special items for prayer and recollection were only part of Wilberforce's attempts to foster an ongoing communion with God,[123] to achieve a continual sense of God's presence.[124] He agreed with Doddridge who said "that when we go on ill in the closet, we commonly do so everywhere else."[125] So he continued to use rules and plans to discipline himself as he had in his first years as a Christian. From June of 1794 until May of 1800 he wrote at the top of each page of his diary headings for the faults he felt himself susceptible to, including wandering in prayer, forgetting about the Holy Spirit, lacking humility and self-denial, and many others.[126] Under each heading he would indicate his daily performance: "indifferent," "little in mind," "middling," "baddish," "very bad," "better," "rather better," "better I hope."[127] The schedules he had used previously were brought back into use to monitor his hours during the summer of 1793, and a journal of time was begun in 1822.[128] In the summer of 1812, when he was fifty-three and had been married for fifteen years, he decided on a new set of rules for his devotional time since he found that the others were no longer proving effective:

> When not unavoidably prevented by company or House of Commons, to take an hour, or at least half an hour, for private devotions, including Scripture reading and meditation, immediately before family prayers…How can I expect a blessing otherwise? Oh let me reform here; it has been my standing sin of late…[129]

Losing ground again, he established a plan for evening devotions ten years later at sixty-three:

> To-day I began the plan, to which by God's grace I mean to adhere, of having my evening private devotions before family prayers. For want of this they have too often been sadly hurried, and the reading of Scriptures omitted. I have therefore resolved to allot an hour…It is a subtraction of the space to be allowed to business, but God seems to require it, and the grand, the only question is, what is God's will? The abridgement of my evening prayers has been a fault with me for years. May God help me to amend it…[130]

He developed a habit of carrying a list with him to look at when he had free moments, a list of motives for humiliation or repentance and for thankfulness.[131] He kept such a list at least before 1817.[132] It contained statements he hoped would provoke him to live a more holy life. He was selfish, he was cold towards those he loved, he was self-indulgent. He loved human approval. He procrastinated:

Consider in detail how deficient in the duties of an MP, father, master, friend, companion, brother. Resolutions broken. Intemperance often. How sinful this when taken to Christ—and to self-extinction, for me a vile ungrateful sinner! Oh, shame, shame![133]

He also used this list to encourage his sense of gratefulness. He wrote that he had been born a wealthy Englishman in the eighteenth century, that he had been elected for MP for York, and that he had been directed to take up Abolition and had been successful at it.[134] Gratitude and shame, he told a friend, were "the most powerful of all motives...to exert myself with augmented earnestness."[135] He wanted to gain both self-abhorrence,[136] so that he would progress spiritually by turning from sin, and develop an appreciation of God and what God had done for him. All of this was done so that he might praise God more sincerely, love God more deeply, commune with God more fully, serve God more devotedly; "True Christians consider themselves not as satisfying some rigorous creditor, but as discharging a debt of gratitude."[137]

It is evident from the foregoing material that many of the habits Wilberforce formed in the months and years immediately following his conversion were sustained throughout the major part of his political career, the years 1789-1824. This is because he had had a penetrating conversion experience in which Doddridge, Milner, and Newton had imbedded Evangelical doctrine deep into his mind and soul. The consequence was Wilberforce did not spend time searching for newer or different doctrines but in seeking to apply and reapply those same doctrines he had already grounded his faith on. The study of his spiritual development becomes less an examination of increasing affinity to Evangelical doctrine than of the various methods Wilberforce employed in order to manifest the implications of those Evangelical truths. It becomes the study of one man's battle to make Evangelicalism a vital force in every aspect of his life. The contents of Wilberforce's *A Practical View of the Prevailing Religious System of Professed Christians*, published in 1797, substantiates this opinion. The doctrine it promulgated was not essentially different from that which

Doddridge, Milner, and Newton had expounded to Wilberforce a decade or more before (see Chapters IV and V). Wilberforce's beliefs had only been buttressed by his reading of evangelical theologians during the interval. This being understood, it will be convenient for the remainder of this section to discuss Wilberforce's spirituality largely along thematic lines, bearing in mind that the development which was occurring in him was the process, by means of spiritual battles lost and won, of translating doctrinal beliefs into a consistent and potent Christian lifestyle.

The publication of *A Practical View* was in fact a watershed in Wilberforce's life. It offered him an opportunity to reflect on and confirm the Evangelical faith that had taken him by storm in 1785. The book became a best-seller and was read widely. It made Wilberforce the key spokesman for the Evangelical Movement. *A Practical View* was his mature thought and he tried to advise others out of his own experience and understanding:

> It is essential...that you guard against the distraction of worldly cares; and cultivate heavenly-mindedness, and a spirit of continual prayer; and that you watch incessantly over the workings of your own deceitful heart. To this I must add, that you must be useful.[138]

Wilberforce practiced what he preached. This section has already discussed a number of ways in which he sought to maintain an active awareness of God's presence: his use of Sundays in solitude, his development of an evening devotional time in addition to a morning one, his selection of birthdays and New Year and other special occasions for periods of prayer and meditation, his careful organization of time so that none of it was wasted that could be given to God. In addition to all of these means Wilberforce made use of life's darker moments to train his mind to stay fixed on God.

For instance, Wilberforce frequently reflected on death. "I have always thought," he said when his eldest daughter died in 1821, "that we should use such seasons for associating spiritual impressions and ideas with the concerns of common life."[139] On the day of the funeral he reviewed his own life, thanked God for his mercy, and committed himself to God afresh: "And now, Lord, let me devote myself more solemnly and more resolutely to Thee, desiring more than I ever yet have done to dedicate my faculties to Thy glory and service."[140]

Wilberforce also meditated on the inevitability of his own death in order to develop the proper "frame of mind" and "course of conduct."[141] He had an acute sense of the day he would face God and be judged—an awareness of personal accountability stirred him to action. It was important for him to be "fit for heaven," because his death could come when he would least expect it, and then there would no longer be an opportunity to make himself worthy to dwell in God's presence: "Let us all remember that if we would be admitted into heaven we must be made meet for it here."[142]

Suffering and the discouraging thoughts that it brought on were also used by Wilberforce to bring his mind to bear on God, for though Wilberforce's temperament was naturally ebullient, he had difficult experiences which depressed him. Invariably, he covered up his discouragement with a cheerful exterior. He wrote to a friend in 1825:

> I sometimes think that I have the art…of concealing from my most intimate associates my real character…I am at times much more disposed to melancholy than you would imagine.[143]

What were some of the reasons for this cheerful and hard-working man's depressions? He took opium for several decades. Long-term side effects include depression and indolence, both of which Wilberforce experienced. The fragility of his body meant that he had more than his share of physical suffering; for the last fifteen or eighteen years of his life he had to wear a steel frame to support his arms and upper torso.[144] His sister and his two daughters died during his lifetime, as well as many close friends. The battle for Abolition was long and full of disappointing turns. He was not always aware of God's support during this drawn-out conflict and he felt that the apparent absences of God keenly.[145] He meditated on his sufferings so that he could gain deeper spiritual insight from them.

He reckoned that his sufferings taught him about "the shortness and uncertainty of all human things."[146] They weaned him from the world.[147] They were sent to give him time for more protracted periods of prayer.[148] God used them to chastise him.[149] God even used them to punish Wilberforce, as in the case of a sickness of his wife which Wilberforce believed God sent to deal with a feeling of exultation he had.[150]

Wilberforce used physical aids to keep his thoughts on God too. He memorized Scripture passages, apparently in Greek as well as in English.[151] He relied on specific Scriptural promises for encouragement.[152] He went so far as to put a pebble in his shoe in an effort to keep spiritual realities on his mind:

> Let me try to keep myself reminded of invisible things by something which will call attention, though not produce pain...I did try a little pebble in my shoe. Why should such secondary means be despised? Oh that they were unnecessary, and so they may become by degrees! Oh may I learn to live above this world, and set my affections on things above.[153]

He even tried his Evangelical equivalent of Jewish phylacteries: "I have used an expedient to the Jewish phylacteries,...in order to keep up the sense of God's presence. Let me try it again."[154] This was the same man who in 1789 had an arrangement going with Isaac Milner where he would forfeit to Milner a certain sum of money every time he exceeded his personal rules.[155] Thirty years later he was still as desperate for God and as anxious to please him. As a mature Christian he pushed himself as hard or harder than he had as a young convert, both in terms of spiritual development and in terms of serving God through his political career. His frequent fasting throughout his life hurt his health.[156] At times his habit of rising early for personal devotions wore him down physically.[157] He cried during his meditations, straining and damaging his weak and delicate eyes.[158] On the other side of the spectrum, frequently he could not take time for prayer and Scripture reading because he was overworked.[159]

Keeping in mind the caution that the Wilberforce of the private confessional was not the gregarious and ebullient Wilberforce the public saw, the fact remains that he worked extremely hard, both inside the prayer closet and out of it, to know and please his God.

When things went well he was still not content, but urged himself to further goals and achievements—Abolition accomplished, he cried:

> When I look back on my parliamentary life, and see how little, all taken together, I have duly adorned in the doctrine of God my Saviour, I am ashamed and humbled in the dust; may any time which remains, Lord, be better employed.[160]

Why did Wilberforce drive himself like this? There were many reasons. Wilberforce was exactly the sort of man who rose to a sense of mission. He had been a highly principled Englishman even before his conversion. It stood to reason that once he believed it was God's will to serve as a member of the British Parliament his strong sense of personal responsibility and accountability would come to the fore. There was also his so-called "mercurial" temperament. It thrived as Wilberforce took on numerous political and public efforts. He seemed to gain energy the more he involved himself in great tasks for God. Then there was the real joy he experienced when he immersed himself in these activities that he felt were pleasing to God. He did not actually like having to be in London and having to be a politician—"How toilsome and unsatisfactory a path is that of politics!"[161]—but he loved it when the fruit of his labors righted injustice, alleviated suffering, or forwarded the cause of Christ in the nation.

It was also important to Wilberforce that his life matter. This was part of his upbringing and of his education as a wealthy young aristocrat. It was encouraged by his political inclinations and associations (such as his friendship with reform-minded Pitt). But it was also reinforced and stimulated by his Evangelical theology and spirituality which told him that he must be useful. Years before Wilberforce became a convert to an Evangelical faith he had wanted a practical religion. The Evangelicals gave it to him and he came into his own.

Wilberforce was also spurred on by his belief that God was a Judge who would one day hold him accountable for the manner in which he had spent his life in God's service. Wilberforce wanted to be ready for the day he faced God and he was acutely aware that his own sin and depravity were constantly drawing him up short of the mark. He knew he must work hard to overcome his sinful inclinations if he was to succeed in any of his endeavors. He read a great deal of the Puritans, men like John Owen, Richard Baxter, John Flavel, John Howe, and the American Puritan Jonathan Edwards (all of whom are discussed in Chapter V), and they passed these beliefs on to him. Along with these doctrines, they passed on a lack of assurance concerning eventual salvation. Wilberforce believed he was saved by the grace of God, yet in practical terms, like John Bunyan's characters in *Pilgrim's Progress*, a book which Wilberforce knew well, there could be no lasting certainty of this until he had "crossed the Jordan" and was actually dwelling in God's presence in heaven.[162] The Calvinistic Puritans looked to prove their election to salvation to themselves by their spiritual fruit. Wilberforce acted in the same way and this became another ingredient which added to the intensity of his pursuit of spiritual maturity:

> Oh let us all strive lest a promise being left us of entering into His rest, any of us should seem to come short of it. But if we give diligence to make our calling and election sure, we never shall, we never can fail…But let us all remember that if we would be admitted hereafter into heaven we must be made meet for it here… 'If any man have not the Spirit of Christ he is none of His.' Oh let this thought quicken our endeavours and our prayers.[163]

This battle for assurance lasted right up to Wilberforce's death. "O then, my soul, strive—to him that overcometh only, the promise is assured,"[164] he wrote in 1829. A year later it was:

> I know I must be near death, perhaps very near it. I believe that on the state in which death find me, will depend my eternal condition; and even though my state may now be such as to produce humble hope that I am safe, yet by a wise improvement of my time, I may augment my eternal happiness…[165]

This need to be sure, perhaps sometimes a fear that his depravity would win out, was a strong motivating force behind his spiritual drive: "Remember, O my soul, that if thou availest not thyself of these warnings, the greater will by they condemnation."[166]

This was a common Evangelical trait. It had arisen in the first place because the Wesleyan Methodists had emphasized that experience was the basis of assurance, thereby practically equating faith and assurance.[167] The Evangelicals had reacted to this by stating that faith was not synonymous with assurance, that it could and did exist alongside doubts and fears about one's salvation.[168] The actual proof of one's faith was seen to be the slow change of a Christian's character.[169] This Evangelical teaching had also come about in reaction to a hyper-Calvinist stress on self-confidence about one's salvation which could lead to Antinomianism.[170] The Evangelicals were careful to walk a fine line between the Wesleyan and the hyper-Calvinist doctrines in this area. Donald Lewis states:

> Their [the Evangelicals'] caution about religious experiences and about religious certitude led them to emphasize the importance of self-doubt and self-questioning.[171]

Thus, Wilberforce's drawn-out and agonized struggles over the state of his soul. There were yet other reasons for the energy and drive so much a part of his spirituality. He could not feel content because his sense of sin and guilt could only be expiated in confession and service. And how else could he show his gratitude to God but by worship and activities performed in God's name? Then too he was a very humble man. "Humility," he wrote, "is indeed the vital principle of Christianity—that principle by which, from first to last, she lives and thrives."[172] This being the case, how could he ever say he had repaid the debt of gratitude he owed to God for sacrificing his only Son for Wilberforce's soul? How much could ever be enough? So Wilberforce pressed on.

The enigma is, all this effort suited him so well. He was not irritable, though he did seem to suffer from the sort of malaise that is associated with a high degree of stress and overwork. He was a man apparently at peace. His sons observed that in 1817:

> A stranger might have noticed little else than that he was more uniformly cheerful than most men of his time of life. Closer observation showed a vein of Christian feeling mingling with

70

and purifying...a most happy temper; whilst those who lived most continually with him, could trace distinctly...the continual presence of that 'peace which the world can neither give nor take away.'[173]

Commenting on Wilberforce's personality a woman remarked: "I should be always cheerful too, if I could make myself as sure as he does that I was going to heaven."[174] His concerns about his salvation and his lack of spiritual progress, his discontent at not being able to serve God as fully as he thought he should, none of this enervated his naturally cheerful disposition. He enjoyed God and he enjoyed life with God and it was this which was actually the strongest inducement to a spiritual life. He loved God and he knew, despite his struggles, that God loved him in Jesus Christ: "The love of God and my Redeemer, that this blessed principle may be like the main-spring of the machine, prompting all the movements, and diffusing its practical influence through every disposition, action, plan, and design."[175]

Even with his strong principles, his voracious appetite for devotional and theological reading, and his powerful sense of building all of his life around a relationship with God sustained by constant and varied religious disciplines, Wilberforce would not have come to his retirement so successful an Evangelical politician without the support of many friends. Wilberforce himself recognized this. He stated that friendship was an important part of a Christian's spiritual development.[176] "I have long thought," he told a good friend in 1811, "that of all the manifold blessings which Providence has heaped on me, the greatest of this world...consists of kind and intelligent friends, whom He has raised up for my comfort and benefit."[177] He found the company of Christian friends the most beneficial.[178] Some of the greatest encouragement came from John Venn and other members of the Clapham Group.

This band of men began to meet regularly in Clapham, then a village a couple of miles outside of London, for mutual support in the Christian life as it related to public service. They usually met on weekends and holidays and their families were constantly with them. There was also a number of friends who joined them from time to time, including Hannah More. This Clapham Group did not exhibit a theological consensus, but they did have in common an Anglican Evangelicalism and a commitment to a "practical Christianity" that worked itself out in areas of philanthropy, education, moral reform, and social reform. They were imbued with the post-millennial optimism that was mentioned in Chapter II, the feeling of being able to establish a Kingdom of God on earth that would last one thousand years and herald the return of Christ. For help in this task they went to the Bible, but not as literalists—instead, they tried to operate in line with the spirit of the Scriptures. Many, like Wilberforce, were concerned not only with the material good they could do, but with the spiritual good. In the social reform they fought to achieve, they hoped they opened a way for those helped to hear the Christian gospel.[179]

When they met they discussed public issues in an Evangelical light. They also dealt with personal problems. Lean states:

> Often they gathered in 'Cabinet Councils' in [Henry] Thornton's library over the public cause or personal needs of the moment, for private as well as public plans were common property between them. They aimed to make every decision on a basis of what, as far as they could see, God desired for the whole fellowship and for the country; they believed this perspective was not best found alone.[180]

Community and frank and sincere Christian fellowship were crucial sustaining forces in Wilberforce's life. The Group remained an important influence during the time it was in existence, from approximately 1792 until 1815. The death of John Venn in 1813 and particularly of Henry Thornton in 1815 (Thornton had owned Battersea Rise in Clapham, the "headquarters" of the Group) inevitably led to its dissolution.

The Period of Retirement (1825-1833)

Wilberforce did not relent from his spiritual regimen after he had retired from politics in 1825. A typical day went something like this: At seven in the morning, ninety minutes of personal devotions; then forty-five minutes of dressing while listening to a reader speak Scripture or some devotional piece out loud; family prayers at nine-thirty, including the reading and exposition of a portion of Scripture by Wilberforce himself; this was followed by a short walk and then breakfast at ten, where he liked to enjoy discussions with friends which might last until noon; then he went to his study to work on his correspondence until post time at three o'clock; at this point he walked in the garden, often reading and reciting from a Psalter or Shakespeare as he strolled; dinner was at five, after which he laid down for ninety minutes—this rest energized him for the long evening of reading, prayer, and conversation in which he belied his growing age; evening prayers occurred around nine o'clock; after this he would usually have someone read to him, typically material of a religious nature; he would not go to bed until midnight or later, and this when he was in his late sixties and early seventies.[181]

He continued to fast, though usually in the sense of abstaining from favorite foods.[182] He continued to have special days for prayer and self-examination, often using his own birthday and the birthdays of his children for such purposes.[183] He continued to read the Bible: "The Psalms, and St. Paul's Epistles, are more and more dear to me."[184] Nature remained the beautiful window to God: "Surely flowers are the smiles of His goodness."[185] The habits ingrained in him over decades of struggle remained with him to bring a great amount of peace and thankfulness. "His overflowing gratitude to God," write his sons, "was the chief feature of his later years."[186] Even a severe financial loss when he was seventy could not shake him. Two days later he calmly set down, "A solitary walk with the psalmist—evening quiet."[187]

To be sure, he had his battles. He was still not content with his religious development, still not sure he would spend his eternity with God.[188] He felt it expedient that he continue to grow Godwards. At seventy-three he said, "You must all join with me in praying that the short remainder of my life may be spent in gaining that spirituality of mind which will fit me for heaven."[189] At his moment of death, in response to his son's encouragement that Wilberforce had his feet "on the Rock," he said, "I do not venture to speak so positively; but I hope I have."[190]

Brown and Furneaux have sided with Wilberforce's sons in claiming that in his old age Wilberforce moved away from Evangelicalism. Furneaux says that by 1828 Wilberforce's Evangelical faith "was fairly muted,"[191] and his interest in High Church Anglicanism had been revived.[192] The evidence cited to support this theory is that he hired a Roman Catholic tutor for his grandson, that he sent his sons to Oxford University with its High Church orientation, and that he did not mind when his sons became High Churchmen so long as they were "truly religious."[193] To this is added the fact that the new generation of Evangelicals was quite different from the first. "Bleak, dour, humourless men," Furneaux calls them, "bigoted, unimaginative, stupid, colourless, and vulgar."[194] Brown concurs:

> It is hard to doubt that from the 1820's on there swarm into the [Evangelical] Party increasing and eventually dominating numbers of a kind of Evangelical that Wilberforce for one did not like.[195]

Indeed, the face of the Evangelical Movement was changing for the worse. The new Evangelicals were not the sort of men who had the vision and the wide scope of concerns both social and evangelistic which the Clapham Group had had. Wilberforce was not happy with this turn of events. "I see much in the state of the world and church," he said two weeks before his death, "which I deplore."[196] Nevertheless, his disappointment with the transformation of the Evangelical Movement hardly amounted to a disappointment with Evangelical doctrine, and the evidence cited by Brown and Furneaux bears a more accurate interpretation.

Wilberforce cared a great deal, as did the other Evangelicals of the first generation of the Movement, for an education that was both broad and penetrating. Therefore, if the best tutor that could be had for his grandson was a Roman Catholic, let the man teach his grandson various subjects. Wilberforce, as shall be seen in Chapter IV, was a man who could talk to a Roman Catholic about Evangelical principles not with a concern to making the man a Protestant but, in fact, a more "truly religious" Catholic.[197] Oriel College, Oxford was chosen for three of Wilberforce's sons over Trinity College, Cambridge for the same reason a Roman Catholic tutor was chosen for his grandson, a better education. Trinity's "numerous, mostly rich and too frequently idle undergraduates" had proved to be the undoing of Wilberforce's eldest son William.[198] Since the next eldest son, Robert, was already showing "intellectual prowess" Wilberforce was concerned that this be properly nurtured.[199] In fact, the sons that went to Oriel all did extremely well academically.[200] As for his sons becoming High Churchmen, it seems evident that he did not see that this was happening. Pollock suggests that "their shift from Evangelical theology was slow enough to be disguised from an adored and adoring father."[201] If Wilberforce did catch hints of this theological shift, it always concerned him, as on the occasion in which Robert delivered a sermon which suggested that conversion to Christ was not a necessity for someone baptized in infancy.[202] If he had lived to see sons of his join the Roman Catholic Church he would have been dismayed. For as broad-minded as he was, he did not like Roman Catholicism. As late as 1831 or 1832, he had written William Jay:

> My motives for supporting what is very ill-entitled Catholic emancipation, were, not that I thought that when granted the Roman Catholics would desire no more; still less, because I did not entertain a very strong repugnance to the Roman Catholic religion of the present day;...[203]

The fact that outside of bending a few pieces of circumstantial evidence to support their own theory, evidence that is quite capable of supporting an opposing opinion, Brown and Furneaux have no evidence for Wilberforce's disavowal of Evangelicalism at all. Wilberforce's own letters and diaries say nothing of it. In fact, they clearly support the opposite contention, that Wilberforce remained a strong Evangelical to the end. "The theory advance by Ford K. Brown and repeatedly by Furneaux," argues Pollock, "that W[ilberforce]'s Evangelicalism became muted at the end of his life finds no support in the MS sources."[204]

Wilberforce did not abandon the faith that had changed his life. He continued to read the Puritans.[205] He continued in his Evangelical spirituality, stressing the importance of the Holy Spirit in his life.[206] He maintained his relationship with non-Anglican evangelicals such as William Jay. Less than two weeks before Wilberforce's death, his wife sent a note to Jay to come and say good-bye. Wilberforce told Jay:

> I see much in the state of the world and church which I deplore, yet I am not among the croakers. I think real religion is spreading; and, I am persuaded, will increasingly spread, till the earth is filled with the knowledge of the Lord, as the waters cover the sea.[207]

Then he added, clutching Jay's hand:

> I am glad you have not turned aside...but have kept to the common, plain, and important truths, in which all Christians are nearly agreed; and I hope you will never leave the good old way:—God bless you![208]

Wilberforce remained an Evangelical, anchored in the faith that had harboured him as a boy and as a man. The essentials he had grasped by the time he published the "Evangelical manifesto" at thirty-seven—*A Practical View*—were never discarded. [209]

Notes

1. Wilberforce, quoted in *Wilberforce and Wilberforce*, 4:346.

2. Ibid., 1:5.

3. For example, ibid., 1:252 and 2:334.

4. Wilberforce, quoted in John Harford, *Recollections of William Wilberforce* (London, 1864), pp. 207, 218, cited by Lean, p. 10.

5. *Wilberforce and Wilberforce*, 1:6.

6. Wilberforce, quoted ibid.

7. *Wilberforce and Wilberforce*, 1:5.

8. Furneaux, p. 5.

9. Furneaux, Foreword to J*ourney to the Lake District from Cambridge*

(1779), by William Wilberforce (Stocksfield: Oriel Press, 1983), pp. 11-12.

10. *Wilberforce and Wilberforce,* 1:5-6.

11. Wilberforce, Wrangham MSS, Aug. 1772, cited by Furneaux, *Wilberforce,* pp. 8-9.

12. Wilberforce, quoted in *Wilberforce and Wilberforce,* 1:6.

13. Ibid.

14. Ibid., 1:8.

15. Wilberforce and Wilberforce, *The Correspondence of William Wilberforce,* 2 vols. (London: John Murray, 1840), 1:56.

16. Wilberforce, quoted in *Wilberforce and Wilberforce, Life,* 16-7.

17. Ibid., 1:25, 1:29, 1:48.

18. Ibid., 1:29.

19. *WDCS,* 1983 ed., s.v. "George Herbert," by Gordon S. Wakefield.

20. Wilberforce, *Journey,* p. 65.

21. Pollock, p. 33.

22. Wilberforce, quoted in *Wilberforce and Wilberforce, Life,* 1:32.

23. Cragg, pp. 139-40.

24. Ibid., p. 117.

25. Ibid.

26. Ibid., p. 133.

27. Pollock, p. 33.

28. Ibid.

29. Ibid., pp. 33-34.

30. Ibid., p. 33.

31. Wilberforce, quoted in *Wilberforce and Wilberforce, Life,* 1:76.

32. Ibid., 1:48.

33. Pollock, p. 66.

34. *The Dictionary of National Biography,* 1949-50 ed., s.v. "Charles Edward De Coetlogon."

35. Wilberforce, quoted in *Wilberforce and Wilberforce, Life*, 1:48.

36. Pollock, p. 32.

37. Ibid., p. 4.

38. Pollock, p. 33.

39. Brown, p. 74.

40. *Wilberforce and Wilberforce, Life*, 1:76.

41. Isaac Milner, quoted in ibid.

42. *Wilberforce and Wilberforce*, ibid., 1:76-77.

43. Pollock, p. 36.

44. Ibid., pp. 7-9.

45. Wilberforce, quoted in Samuel Wilberforce, "Fragments of his Father's Conversation," p. 122, cited by Pollock, p. 36.

46. Wilberforce, quoted in Wilberforce and Wilberforce, *Life*, 1:87.

47. Ibid., 1:88.

48. Ibid.

49. Ibid.

50. Ibid., 1:89.

51. Ibid.

52. These men are discussed at the end of Chapter V. Pascal was a French Catholic writer and Butler an Anglican bishop.

53. Pollock, p. 38.

54. Wilberforce, quoted in Wilberforce and Wilberforce, *Life*, 1:93.

55. Ibid.

56. Lean, p. 35.

57. Wilberforce, quoted in Wilberforce and Wilberforce, *Life*, 1:97.

58. Ibid., 1:108.

59. Pollock, p. 35.

60. Wilberforce, quoted in Wilberforce and Wilberforce, *Life*, 1:105.

61. *WDCS*, 1983 ed., s.v. "Evangelical Spirituality," by Michael Hennell.

62. Wilberforce, quoted in Wilberforce and Wilberforce, *Life*, 1:88.

63. See A.T.S. James, "Philip Doddridge: His Influence on Personal Religion," in Geoffrey F. Nuttall, ed., *Philip Doddridge* (London: Independent Press, 1951), p. 37.

64. Philip Doddridge, *The Rise and Progress of Religion in the Soul* (Glasgow: Chalmers & Collins, 1825), pp. 318-20.

65. Wilberforce, quoted in Wilberforce and Wilberforce, *Life*, 1:116-117.

66. Ibid., 1:117.

67. Ibid., 1:117-118.

68. Ibid., 1:120.

69. Ibid., 1:120-1.

70. Ibid., 1:120.

71. Ibid., 1:122.

72. Ibid., 1:128.

73. Ibid., 1:123.

74. Doddridge, pp. 318 ff., 343 ff.; *WDCS*, 1983 ed., s.v. "Puritan Spirituality," by N.H. Keeble.

75. Wilberforce, quoted in Wilberforce and Wilberforce, *Life*, 1:122.

76. Ibid., 1:112.

77. William Haller, *The Rise of Puritanism* (Philadelphia: University of Pennsylvania Press, 1938), p. 100.

78. *WDCS*, 1983 ed., s.v. "Spiritual Journal," by Francis Dorff.

79. Ibid.

80. Ibid.

81. *WDCS*, 1983 ed., s.v. "John Wesley," by R.W. Gribben.

82. See Robert C. Monk, *John Wesley: His Puritan Heritage* (Nashville: Abingdon Press, 1966), p. 174.

83. Ibid., p. 175, n. 22.

84. John Wesley, *The Journal of the Rev. John Wesley, A.M.*, ed. Nehemiah Curnock, vol. 1 (London: Epworth Press, 1909), pp. 42-44, cited "the same place."

85. *WDCS*, 1983 ed., s.v. "Methodist Spirituality," by R.W. Gribben.

86. *WDCS*, 1983 ed. s.v. "Evangelical Spirituality," by Michael Hennell.

87. Pollock, p. 45.

88. Lean, p. 39; Mrs. Sykes, quoted in Wilberforce and Wilberforce, *Life*, 1:119, cited by Lean, p. 39.

89. Pollock, p. 66.

90. Wilberforce, Lincolnshire Papers, letter to Lord Carrington, 17 Aug. 1829, cited by Pollock, p. 46.

91. Pollock, p. 69.

92. Quoted in Wilberforce and Wilberforce, *Life*, 1:169.

93. Pollock, p. 81.

94. Wilberforce, "March, 1788," cited "the same place."

95. Ibid., p. 82.

96. Ibid.

97. Ibid.

98. Wilberforce, quote in Wilberforce and Wilberforce, *Life*, 1:182.

99. Ibid.

100. Coupland, p. 187.

101. Wilberforce's schedules, quoted in Wilberforce and Wilberforce, *Life*, 1:194.

102. Ibid.

103. Ibid., 1:195.

104. Ibid., 1:193. Anthony Horneck (1641-1697) immigrated to England from his home on the Rhine in 1661. He became the bishop of Linden and was a popular preacher. The rules which Wilberforce was using may have been the rules Horneck set down for a society for the reformation of manners he helped to found. The rules were printed in Bishop Kidder's *The Life of Anthony Horneck*, published in 1698 (pp. 13-16). This seems likely, but Wilberforce may have been using rules from Horneck's *The Happy Ascetik: or, The Best Exercise*, first published in London in 1686. A sixth edition of this work was published in London in 1724. See *DNB*, 1949-50 ed., s.v. "Anthony Horneck."

105. Ibid., 1:208.

106. Ibid., 1:202.

107. Henry Foster, William Romaine, and John Newton have been identified earlier in the biography. Thomas Scott was an Evangelical and Calvinistic preacher and Bible commentator who became chaplain at Lock Chapel in 1785. Richard Cecil was another Evangelical who ministered at St. John's Chapel, Bedford Row from 1780-1808. Balleine called him "the most cultured and refined of all the Evangelical leaders." Balleine, p. 44.

108. Wilberforce, quoted in Wilberforce and Wilberforce, *Life*, 5:143.

109. *WDCS*, 1983 ed., s.v. "Evangelical Spirituality," by Michael Hennell.

110. See John Wigley, *The Rise and Fall of the Victorian Sunday* (Manchester: University Press, 1980), p. 28.

111. Wilberforce, quoted in Wilberforce and Wilberforce, *Life*, 3:266.

112.. Ibid., 2:451-2.

113. Ibid., 3:157.

114. Ibid., 1:337-8.

115. Ibid., 3:425.

116. Ibid., 2:56, 3:122, 3:127.

117. Ibid., 1:241.

118. Ibid., 3:534.

119. Ibid., 2:4.

120. Ibid., 5:6.

121. *WDCS*, 1983 ed., s.v. "Evangelical Spirituality," by Michael Hennell.

122. Marianne Thornton, letter to her sister Henrietta, 1826, cited by E.M. Forster, *Marianne Thornton* (London: Arnold, 1956), pp. 137-8.

123. Wilberforce, quoted in *Wilberforce and Wilberforce, Life*, 4:45.

124. Ibid., 4:139.

125. Ibid., 4:92.

126. Wilberforce, Diary, Wrangham MSS, cited by Furneaux,

Wilberforce, p. 145.

127. Ibid.; Wilberforce also used a system of secret markings mentioned in Wilberforce and Wilberforce, *Life*, 4:342.

128. Wilberforce, quoted in Wilberforce and Wilberforce, *Life*, 2:36, 5:132.

129. Ibid., 4:81.

130. Ibid., 5:132.

131. Ibid., 4:345.

132 Ibid.

133. Ibid., 4:344.

134. Ibid., 4:346.

135. Ibid., 5:31.

136. Ibid., 4:345.

137. Wilberforce, *A Practical View of the Prevailing Religious System of Professed Christians, in the Higher and Middle Classes in this Country, Contrasted with Real Christianity* (Edinburgh: Johnstone and Hunter, n.d.), p. 349.

138. Ibid., p. 348.

139. Wilberforce, quoted in Wilberforce and Wilberforce, *Life*, 5:111.

140. Ibid., 5:114.

141. Ibid., 1:331.

142. Ibid., 4:275.

143. Ibid., 5:227-8.

144. Pollock, p. 234.

145. Wilberforce, quoted in Wilberforce and Wilberforce, *Life*, 5:171.

146. Ibid., 3:355.

147. Ibid., 5:7.

148. Ibid., 2:339.

149. Ibid., 2:380, 382.

150. Ibid., 2:294.

151. Ibid., 3:127, 5:68.

152. Ibid., 4:301, 4:363.

153. Ibid., 3:495.

154. Ibid., 4:84, 4:342-3.

155. Ibid., 1:233.

156. Ibid., 2:351.

157. Ibid., 2:23.

158. Ibid., 4:364.

159. Ibid., 1:207, 1:328, 4:92.

160. Ibid., 3:339.

161. Ibid., 3:429.

162. Ibid., 5:357.

163. Ibid., 4:275.

164. Ibid., 5:323-4.

165. Ibid., 5:324.

166. Ibid., 1:251-2.

167. Donald M. Lewis, "The Evangelical Mission to the British Working Class: A Study of the growth of Anglican support for a pan-evangelical approach to evangelism, with special reference to London, 1828-1860" (Ph.D. thesis, University of Oxford, 1981), p. 64.

168. Ibid.

169. Ibid.

170. Lewis, p. 66.

171. Ibid.

172. Wilberforce, *A Practical View*, p. 346.

173. Wilberforce and Wilberforce, *Life*, 4:339.

174. Quoted ibid., 4:340.

175. Wilberforce, quoted ibid., 3:356.

176. Ibid., p. 210.

177. Wilberforce, quoted in Wilberforce and Wilberforce, *Life*,

3:538.

178. Ibid., 5:292.

179. Wilberforce, quoted in Wilberforce and Wilberforce, *Life*, 4:126.

180. Lean, p. 95.

181. Wilberforce and Wilberforce, *Life*, 5:283ff.

182. Wilberforce, quoted ibid., 5:324.

183. Ibid.

184. Ibid., 5:311.

185. Ibid., 5:287.

186. Ibid., 5:334.

187. Ibid., 5:311.

188. Ibid., 5:324.

189. Ibid., 5:365.

190. Ibid., 5:373.

191. Furneaux, *Wilberforce*, p. 436.

192. Ibid., p. 427.

193. Ibid., p. 428; see also Brown, pp. 500-1.

194. Furneaux, *Wilberforce*, p. 427.

195. Brown, p. 518.

196. Wilberforce, quoted in Jay, p. 317.

197. Wilberforce, Private Papers, pp. 275-6, cited by Furneaux, *Wilberforce*, p. 321.

198. Pollock, p. 278.

199. Ibid.

200. Ibid., p. 297.

201. Ibid., p. 298.

202. Ibid.

203. Wilberforce, quoted in Jay, p. 305.

204. Pollock, p. 348, n. 16.

205. Wilberforce, quoted in Wilberforce and Wilberforce, *Life*,

5:249.

206. Ibid.

207. Wilberforce, quoted in Jay, p. 317.

208. Ibid., p. 314.

209. See Cragg. p. 155, who regards Wilberforce's book as "the most influential manifesto of the Evangelical party."

CHAPTER IV

The Heart of Wilbeforce's Spirituality

Its Evangelical and Puritan Roots

Wilberforce had an Evangelical theology—it was conservative and it centred upon soteriology, emphasizing the need of redemption from original sin and the work of the Holy Spirit in conversion and sanctification.[1] He was not interested in speculative theology, agreeing with Hannah More who said of one work:

> That boldly prying into the awful mysteries of judgment over which the Bible has drawn such an impenetrable veil, I read with more pain than profit...It brought to my mind some lines...'He made hell for such as were too curious, and would know too much.'[2]

Wilberforce liked biblically-based teaching that was applicable to the Christian's daily life. He was, after all, "a pilgrim and a stranger; a soldier,"[3] passing through a world which was but "the antechamber of the next."[4] He needed guidance with which to make the journey and weapons with which to fight. He needed to be as useful as possible in the service of God during the short passage, so he demanded a practical theology. Moreover, with the passage being so brief and people's eternal destinies being at stake, it was only natural that he, like other Evangelicals, should require a theology that emphasized the spiritual over the temporal: "O remember that the salvation of one soul is of more worth than the mere temporal happiness of thousands or even millions."[5] But Brown goes too far when he suggests that the only reason Wilberforce and the Evangelicals took up the cause of the slaves was in order to clear the way for missionaries and to bring the Evangelicals Movement into the limelight.[6] Wilberforce and the others had a real hatred for slavery, temporal as physical suffering might be:

> Pity, anger, indignation, shame, create quite a tumult in my breast, and I feel myself to be criminal for having remained silent so long, and not having sooner proclaimed the wrongs of the negro slaves, and the injustice and oppression of our countrymen.[7]

Brown forgets that both "disinterested love" (loving without ulterior motivation) and ministering to others' needs as Christ had done were crucial elements of Evangelical teaching. "We are commanded," Wilberforce said, "to imitate Him who came not to be ministered unto but to minister."[8]

The Evangelical doctrines Wilberforce espoused in *A Practical View of the Prevailing Religious System of Professed Christians*, as mentioned previously, may be taken as indicative of the beliefs he held throughout his Christian life—his journals and diaries constantly reflect what he wrote there. Wilberforce would go so far as to confront friends and Evangelical ministers if they did not toe the line of essential Evangelical beliefs. "I have then," he wrote William Jay in 1803, "(to come to the point,) been told from various quarters, that your general strain of preaching has been of late not sufficiently Evangelical."[9]

He held to the authority of Scripture,[10] the fallenness and depravity of humankind (which resulted also in the corruption of reason and conscience),[11] original sin,[12] the reality of a personal adversary called Satan,[13] and a place of eternal judgment called Hell.[14] He believed in Christ's substitutionary atonement for humankind's sin,[15] in Christ's resurrection from the dead,[16] that a person was justified before God by grace through faith in Christ alone.[17] Regeneration was essential and the Holy Spirit had to dwell in a believer.[18] He held to unlimited atonement—he was not a thorough-going Calvinist. "Every year that I live," he said when he was sixty-three, "I become more impressed with the unscriptural character of the Calvinistic system."[19] Obviously Wilberforce did not reject all Calvinistic teaching if he believed in human depravity, the substitutionary atonement, salvation by God's grace, justification by faith, the doctrine of providence and the sovereignty of God, not to mention his enjoyment of the writings of Calvinistic Puritans such as John Owen, John Flavel, and Jonathan Edwards and Calvinistic preachers such as John Newton and Thomas Scott. What seemed to offend him was a cold and intellectual Calvinistic interpretation of God and his ways that appeared to leave no room for the mysteries of God and providence and the fallibility of human reason. He said after reading a piece by the London Evangelical and Calvinist preacher William Romaine: "Oh how unlike this is to the Scripture! He writes as if he had sat at the Council Board with the Almighty!"[20] It should also be remembered that, as discussed in the last chapter, the Evangelicals had good reason to be wary of hyper-Calvinist teaching, particularly in the area of faith and assurance. Moreover, as an Evangelical, Wilberforce had inherited the trait of theological toleration developed after the Calvinist-Arminian controversy of the 1770's by men such as Henry Venn, John Venn, and Charles Simeon.[21] They wanted to show the Anglican Church that Evangelicalism was based on Scripture and confirmed by the *Articles and Prayer Book of the Church of England*, not by John Calvin's *Institutes of the Christian Religion*. All of this mitigated against Wilberforce declaring himself or even considering himself a Calvinist though he held to a number of Calvinistic emphases.

The doctrine of providence was important to Wilberforce's thinking: "How I abhor that word, fortunate; as if things happened by chance!"[22] He believed providence existed on a personal and a national scale to save the good and punish the wicked. Thus, he felt God would give a person specific guidance, placing a thought into a person's head as had happened with the Old Testament prophets, with Paul, with Ananias and many others in the book of Acts. He trusted God to help him by supplying him with the right words to speak in Parliament.

And he looked to see God's workings among the nations (musing that Napoleon's return from exile was God's judgment of the continuing apostasy of European nations and England herself).[23]

The framework of national blessings and cursings within which the Evangelicals' concept of providence worked was a pattern they kept sharp note of. God was a retributive God. Wilberforce wrote copiously in his letters and diaries of how God punished the sins of nations. "Our national sins," he wrote a friend in 1796, "force themselves into my mind. Would to God I could see any symptoms of national humiliation."[24] Napoleon and his army was God's tool of judgment on the sins of England and other European countries.[25] England would be punished as a nation for perpetuating the sin of the slave trade.[26] By the same token, however, God would reward the righteousness of nations. Thus, when Britain ended the slave trade in 1807, Wilberforce knew God would smile upon her. "God will bless this country," he said immediately afterward. "The first authentic account of the defeat of the French has come today."[27]

Wilberforce was a patriot, but he did not believe his nation came before God. Rather, if his nation was to prosper, he realized that it must act in accordance with God's decrees. A military victory might be a sign of God's blessing or it might be a sinful act that would provoke God's curse. Wilberforce felt that some wars were necessary and that God used them to work his will,[28] but he did not believe Britain had a divine right to wage war and seize territory. Since God's claims came before the claims of Wilberforce's country, it was conceivable to him that the two sets of claims could just as easily be mutually exclusive as providentially bound together:

> If by patriotism is meant that mischievous and domineering quality which renders men ardent to promote, not the happiness, but the aggrandizement of their own country, by the oppression and conquest of every other—to such patriotism… that religion must be indeed an enemy whose foundation is justice, and whose compendious character is 'peace' and good-will towards men.[29]

It was extremely important to be able to discern and interpret the workings of providence accurately. Not only the destiny of England was at stake, but that of the entire world. After all, the Evangelicals' post-millennial eschatology, which Wilberforce shared, hinged on such signs as the providential operations of God afforded. They believed that Christ's spiritual rule over a righteous and Christian earth was imminent and that the actions of nations could either speed or hinder the dawn of this divine government.[30] They wanted England to be reformed in order to bring about Christ's return and so they went at this task with great zeal. They knew the world had to be reformed before Christ would return and so they set about this task with an equal zeal. Ervine comments:

> The millennial glory was to be ushered in not by miracle, but by the process of world conversion through human means—the Bible and missionary societies of Britain.[31]

In Wilberforce's day, the providential signs of Christ's return seemed clear enough: Pope Pius VII was removed from the Vatican in 1809, Napoleon was defeated at Waterloo in 1815, Roman Catholicism and unbelief were on the wane, and missionary societies for both Jew and Gentile were active.[32] But providence often operated mysteriously and Wilberforce could not always understand its ways. In 1793 he wrote: "Through God's help got the East India Resolutions in quietly."[33] These resolutions were an attempt on Wilberforce's part to see that the East India Company allowed the widespread operation of Christian missionaries in India (the powerful mercantile company had virtual control of Britain's interests in India). What could seem more suited to God's designs and subsequent support than these resolutions? Yet when he returned to his journal a few days later he had to pen, "How mysterious, how humbling, are the dispensations of God's providence! I see that I closed with speaking of the East India clauses being carried, of which I have now to record the defeat."[34] He found comfort in a deeper understanding of the workings of providence which he expressed in *A Practical View* four years later:

It must be a solid support to us amidst all our troubles, to know, that they do not happen to us by chance; that they are not even merely the punishment of sin; but that they are the dispensations of a kind of Providence, and sent as messages of mercy.[35]

A good Anglican, Wilberforce had a place in his theology for the importance of the liturgy, and the sacraments of Eucharist and child baptism, differing with other Anglicans in his belief that there were other means of grace besides the discipline and sacraments of the Church of England—the Bible and preaching, to name two.[36] He was also adamant in declaring that a true Anglican faith had to be based on what he called "vital Christianity"[37]—Evangelical doctrines: "This is the very Christianity on which our Establishment is founded; and that which her Articles, and Homilies, and Liturgy, teach throughout."[38]

Nevertheless, important as Evangelical theology was to Wilberforce, it was important only as the proper foundation to a life lived in the service of God. It was the stepping stone to what really counted—a fervent spirituality lived out in the world:

The grand characteristic mark of the true Christian…is his desiring to please God in all his thoughts, and words, and actions; to take the revealed Word to be the rule of his belief and practice; to 'let his light shine before men;' and in all things to adorn the doctrine which he professes.[39]

A Puritan Spirituality

The second aspect which went to make up the core of William Wilberforce's religious thought was a vibrant spirituality largely comprised of English Puritan emphases. In 1797 Wilberforce said that the writings of the English Puritans were "prolix" and too sub-divided, "yet they are a mine of wealth, in which anyone who will submit to some degree of labour, will find himself well rewarded for his pains."[40] Their influence is obvious in his thinking as was pointed out during the study of Wilberforce's religious development in Chapter III. If his spirituality needed to be summed up in one word, "Puritan" would be the most accurate. In fact, he was attacked for being a Puritan by the Rev. Robert Fellows in the latter's *Picture of Christian Philosophy*.[41] Even though Wilberforce was not a strict Calvinist the title "Puritan" is still appropriate for him if it is recalled that not all the Puritans were strict Calvinists either. N.H. Keeble comments:

> Puritan doctrine was as varied as Puritan ecclesiology. Many Puritans, such as [John] Owen and John Bunyan…did retain the Calvinist allegiance of the Puritan fathers, the 'English Calvin' William Perkins…and William Ames…, but others, like Tobias Crisp…, so stressed the unmerited free grace of Christ as to be denounced by Calvinists as antinomians….There were such divines as John Goodwin…who rejected Calvinism for Arminianism. Some, like [Richard] Baxter, favoured the 'middle way' of Moise Amyraut's 'hypothetical universalism', while Peter Sterry…could combine Calvinism with Cambridge Platonism. The courageous intellectual independence of Puritanism encompassed disciples of Jakob Boehme…, the heterodox theology of John Milton…and the unitarianism of John Biddle…[42]

Like the Puritans, Wilberforce was criticized for trying to legislate his brand of piety and morality. His formation of a Society for the Better Observance of Sunday falls under this criticism. So does the formation of the Proclamation Society to encourage the enforcement of a royal edict, the Proclamation for the Encouragement of Piety and Virtue and for the Preventing of Vice, Profaneness and Immorality, reissued by George III on June 1, 1787. Such actions were predictable, for like the Puritans, Wilberforce was concerned with living out his spirituality in a way which would affect all areas of life, not just the manner in which he prayed in his room or the way he raised his children. The penal system, the number of crimes punishable by hanging, the integrity of English magistrates, dueling, lotteries, drunkenness, Sabbath-breaking—everything had to be influenced. This was a main theme of Evangelical spirituality, that the Christian faith must "be carried into every corner of life and allowed to fill it."[43] But Wilberforce, like the best of English Puritans, was no legalist, no self-righteous bigot. However much others might disagree with his morality and his endeavour to re-create England in the image of that morality, they never saw him as a religious hypocrite. Coupland writes:

> Surely he was a prig? Well, the answer is the old answer—his contemporaries did not think so. There were others than the slave-traders...who disliked Wilberforce, hated his politics, railed at his religion; but none of them seems to have regarded him as arrogant or insincere.[44]

Like the Puritans, Wilberforce saw the enjoyment of public amusements as an indication of a person's spiritual shallowness. He shunned the theatre because of the immorality that attached itself to it, describing it as "pernicious"[45] and admonishing his sister, "Will not, then, your presence at the amusements of the theatre sanction them in the minds of all who you see there?"[46] He tried to avoid playing cards, he felt uncomfortable about dancing (though he did not mind domestic dancing),[47] and he disapproved of horse racing. He did not mention art or artists in his papers, nor were the poems of John Keats, Percy Bysshe Shelley, or Samuel Coleridge ever discussed (though Wilberforce was a good friend of William Wordsworth).[48] As with his music, Wilberforce enjoyed the religious theme best when it came to literature and concentrated on the works of William Cowper and John Milton. Yet he made room for Shakespeare, the adventure novels of Walter Scott, and the Greek and Latin Classics. Nevertheless, he appeared satisfied only if a book was directly spiritual or ethical or increased his knowledge of a particular subject. Since music was enjoyed along these lines, it meant that the Hallelujah Chorus brought Wilberforce to tears, but when a friend asked him to a concert that would take place in the morning, he exclaimed: "Music in the morning! It would be as bad as dram-drinking."[49]

The Evangelicals did not like the pastimes enjoyed by the fashionable.[50] At the same time they, for the most part, enjoyed materially comfortable life styles, even though they were great philanthropists. Hannah More declared that piety was not at war with elegance.[51] Evangelicals felt it was wrong to dress beneath one's station and Wilberforce, who had to move daily among the rich and powerful, believed it wrong to be eccentric and dress less than adequately for social occasions. But Wilberforce did not like the image of the cultured gentleman that many in the Evangelical Movement conveyed. He lived a simpler life style, below what his money and station afforded him, regretting "that many Evangelicals did not live less comfortably and give more to the cause."[52]

The Evangelicals, children of the Puritans, renounced the world and its idle, casual approach to life while they sat back and enjoyed their material possessions. Rosman states that criticism has been leveled at this point "not so much against their enjoyment of worldly comforts as against their theological disparagement of that enjoyment."[53] The pleasure found in material objects was always depreciated because it had to be subordinated to higher spiritual goals. Wilberforce was locked into this way of thinking. In 1818 one of his children asked him why he did not buy a summer home in the Lake District that he loved so much. He replied:

> I should enjoy it as much as anyone, my dear, but we must remember we are not sent into the world merely to admire prospects and enjoy scenery. We have nobler objects of pursuit…Now and then when we need rest from severe labours, it may be permitted us to luxuriate in such lonely spots, but it is to fit us for a return to duty…We may be contented to wait for full enjoyment till we get to that blessed place…[54]

This exactly reflects the Puritan understanding of the place of the material world in a Christian's spirituality, as M.M Knappen notes:

> The Puritans did not oppose pleasure as such, which they admitted was necessary in moderation to refresh the body, but objected to it if it exceeded this essential minimum and hence took time and energy which might be devoted to better ends.[55]

The rejection of worldly indulgence went along with the Evangelical emphasis that life was serious, that gravity and a sober-minded attitude were to be preferred to levity and trifling. This made some of them look askance at a Christian who might be too cheerful. Hannah More said that Wilberforce had "as much wit as if he had no piety."[56] Yet she also advised him: "You are serving God by making yourself agreeable...to worldly but well-disposed people, who would never be attracted to religion by grave and severe divines."[57] Wilberforce sought, in his own words "to preserve a constant and sober mind with a gay exterior."[58] His bright and outgoing personality was always tempered with an understanding that life was serious business, a spiritual warfare. This concept, along with a vision of life as pilgrimage, was another Puritan motif.

So it is too easy to think that because Puritans and Evangelicals slighted "non-religious matter in order to emphasize the over-riding importance of things spiritual" that they had little joy.[59] Gravity was not to be indulged in any more than levity, for as Wilberforce wrote of the Christian, "Let neither his joys intoxicate, nor his sorrows too much depress him."[60] Joy was the very mark of Wilberforce's spirituality, a joy centred not in creature comforts but in spiritual realities. An hour spent with God in prayer was more enjoyable in Wilberforce's estimation than three or four hours of food and conversation at the sort of extended dinner parties prevalent among the wealthy and influential. He was excited about being close to God. For him, as for the Puritans, religion was not a set of rules but "a life-force: a vision and compulsion which saw the beauty of a holy life and moved towards it, marveling at the possibilities and thrilling to the satisfaction of a God-centred life."[61]

Wilberforce wanted to be "fit for heaven." Everything, including recreation, had to serve this important goal. His longing for heaven was no opiate. Personal holiness did not supercede his sense of social mission, of doing good in the earthly realm. He was an inheritor of the same cultural morality as the Puritans, a medieval one which was community-minded, thinking of society first and then the individual as part of that society. Neither the Puritans nor Wilberforce separated concern for personal holiness from concern for national holiness and national reform. Puritan spirituality did not consist of isolation from the world and abstention from all that was a part of material reality. Keeble states:

> Iconoclasm, rigid Sabbatarianism, anti-intellectualism and Philistinism were...comparatively rare. The main thrust of Puri-

tan thought was that the way to perfection lay not through absti-
nence and asceticism, but through the right admission and moderate utilization of the world and the flesh. The Puritan neither
under-valued nor over-valued them: he sanctified them.[62]

Wilberforce's spirituality was no different.

Seeking God and heaven, and seeking to be adequate for both
before his death, Wilberforce, like many Puritans, read the Bible,
relied on a good conscience, read practical religious literature, used
diaries and journals for the purpose of self-examination. He prayed
and meditated, preferring, like the Puritans, spontaneous prayer to
formal prayer.[63] He admitted that he enjoyed personal prayer over
group prayer.[64] He tried to achieve an attitude of constant prayer
"without interruption to his labours," interposing "occasional
thoughts of things unseen."[65]

Wilberforce hated it when prayer was neglected: "There is nothing
more fatal to the life and power of religion; nothing which makes God
more certainly withdraw his grace."[66] Meditation was equally essential:
"Rise on the wings of contemplation…[so that back at work you] act
as in the presence of an 'innumerable company of angels, and of spirits
of just men made perfect, and of God the Judge of all.'"[67] Wilberforce
wanted to "acquire a habit" of living under the influence of the
invisible.[68] So he fasted and kept in the company of sincere Christians
as much as possible and formed friendship with godly men and
women. This too had been an aspect of Puritan spirituality. Personal
relationships were rarely superficial between Puritans and contributed
greatly in areas of confession, encouragement, and self-knowledge.[69]

The family was important to the Puritans. It was important to the
Evangelicals and to Wilberforce too. "My own soul should doubtless
be my first object," he said, "and combined with it my children."[70] He
resigned his influential Yorkshire seat for a lesser one in order to be
closer to his family. He did not drown his children in religion: "They
[parents] should labour to render religion as congenial as possible."[71]
He considered the example he and his wife set crucial to their spiritual
development:

> As I have often said, let it be with us an argument for growing in grace, that in proportion as we do thus cultivate an interest… in the court of Heaven, the more we shall insure our children's edification in answer to our earnest prayers.[72]

The atmosphere in which the six children were raised at Clapham was not dull. They not only were present at family devotions, but enjoyed puppet plays written and performed by various parents, magic lantern shows, and were allowed to "dress up" using Wilberforce's formal attire.[73] They were treated as adults, "a long established upper and middle class habit,"[74] and Wilberforce soon began to long for "decisive marks" of the "great change" in each of them.[75] He wrote to them when he was away on business and continued to keep up with them when they got older and left home for school or marriage. As might be expected, he did not just chat, but turned his letters to serve higher purposes, such as advising a son on the importance of maintaining a morning prayer time.[76]

Wilberforce corresponded with family and close friends and also had mail from all sorts of people on both business and spiritual matters. "I cannot even read during the day," he said in 1815, "all the letters which the morning's post has heaped on me."[77] In 1823 he wrote:

> Alas! I must lessen my correspondence. On looking back through the last year, what else have I done but write letters? Lord, help me to glorify Thee more. I must select, and only write to those who may fairly claim answers. Yet Christianity requires courtesy.[78]

Like the Puritan pastor, Wilberforce was a physician of the soul, and his published letters show him counseling religious contemplation and Bible reading,[79] abstention from habitual preoccupation with "the vanities of this world,"[80] the conquest of false desires by endeavouring "to supplant the fondness of them by the love of better things,"[81] the preservation of a "tenderness of conscience."[82] He advised that the presence of doubt in one individual had a biological or physical source "rather than a refusal of assent to the truth of Christianity,"[83] spoke against the sinfulness of self-sufficiency,[84] promoted the effectiveness of prayers,[85] and the importance of public worship.[86] He counseled the place for obeying God's commands even if a person did not "feel" like it,[87] the importance of believing in and understanding God's grace towards the believer as a weapon against depression,[88] that "perhaps the best way" of getting rid of doubts about the Christian faith "is to act as though they did not exist."[89] He taught that all the dispensations of God, even the most difficult ones, were for the improvement of a person's moral condition.[90] The letters were often written in sterner tone, a little like the attitude he took when admonishing himself in his diary. But, as Furneaux comments:

> It was an Evangelical convention that every letter from one "serious" person to another should include religious sentiment, and it was almost a compliment to criticize or point out the faults of your correspondent.[91]

Evangelism was one of Wilberforce's major concerns, a product as much of his Puritan reading as the Evangelical emphasis on soteriology mentioned in Chapter I. Soon after his conversion in 1785, Wilberforce's sister and a few cousins became Christians as a result of his ministrations. He had a "Friends' Paper" which he looked over each Sunday. It listed a number of friends along with suggestions as to the best way "to help each to take the next step towards a fully satisfying experience with Christ."[92] He also thought out and kept in his mind a number of "conversation directors" against an occasion, public or private, when he might use them to direct a particular individual's thoughts into spiritual matters. In fact, he did become instrumental in the conversion of several friends and politicians, including Matthew Montagu, MP, and Lord Muncaster. Foreign missions was also a matter of great concern. To that end he laboured to see that Christian missionaries would be allowed into India and he helped found the British and Foreign Bible Society so that the Bible and its Gospel message would be promulgated throughout Britain's colonies.

Influenced by John Newton, Philip Doddridge, and especially the Puritan Richard Baxter (see Chapter V), Wilberforce was one with the spirit of interdenominationalism. The difference between Anglican Evangelicals and Dissenting evangelicals was discussed in Chapter I. Wilberforce preferred to remain within the Church of England and he would like to have seen the Dissenters return to its fold. But this did not stop him from recognizing how much all evangelicals had in common. He told his Dissenting friend William Jay:

> Though I am an Episcopalian by education and conviction, I yet feel such a oneness and sympathy with the cause of God at large, that nothing would be more delightful than my communing, once every year, with every Church that holds the Head, even Christ.[93]

No staunch Calvinist, he championed the claims of Calvinist clergy for bishoprics. He could do this because he was a man who believed in religious tolerance, because he was a Christian ecumenist ahead of his time:

> God knows...that it has been...and shall be more and more my endeavour to promote the cordial and vigorous and systematical exertions of all friends of the essentials of Christianity, softening prejudices, healing divisions and striving to substitute a rational and an honest zeal for fundamentals, in place of a hot party spirit.[94]

This spirit of tolerance is one of the salient features of Wilberforce's spirituality. He "took the sacrament" [of Eucharist] at least two times in non-Anglican churches.[95] He fought for Catholic Emancipation in England. Even though he found the Roman Catholicism of his day repugnant,[96] he wrote at one point about "endeavouring to press on him [a person he met at Bath] the most important doctrines of true Christianity and of showing where the case is really so that he may embrace those doctrines and still continue a good Catholic."[97] He was excited about an anniversary meeting of the Bible Society he had helped to form, "five or six hundred people of all sects and parties, with one heart and face and tongue."[98] When his book, *A Practical View*, was published it raised his stature in the Nonconformist or Dissenting churches, strengthening a relationship many found hard to swallow: "They think I cannot be loyal to the Established Church because I love Dissenters."[99]

Remarkably balanced, Wilberforce's spirituality is that of a man who both looked forward to his future communion with God in heaven, and who felt he must act for God during his earthly lifetime. An Anglican who was a friend to all who focused on the essentials of the Evangelical faith, he was also a Puritan enamored of the benefits of a life totally consecrated to God and bodily hurled out into his service. "Let him still remember," he said of the Christian, "that his chief business, while on earth, is not to meditate, but to act."[100]

Notes

1. Rosman, pp. 10-12.

2. Hannah More, quoted in Wilberforce and Wilberforce, *Life*, 5:190; for Wilberforce's letter of response and agreement, 5:210.

3. Wilberforce, *A Practical View*, p. 349.

4. Rosman, p. 55.

5. Wilberforce, quoted in Wilberforce and Wilberforce, *Life*, 4:206.

6. See Brown, pp. 380ff.

7. Wilberforce, quoted in Wilberforce and Wilberforce, *Life*, 5:164.

8. Ibid., 4:389.

9. Wilberforce, quoted in Jay, p. 299.

10. Wilberforce, *A Practical View*, p. iv.

11. Ibid., pp. 22, 23, 32.

12. Ibid., pp. 31, 32, 339.

13. Ibid., p. 32.

14. Ibid., p. 228.

15. Ibid., pp. 50-1.

16. Ibid., p. 54.

17. Ibid., pp. 256-7.

18. Ibid., pp. 51, 233.

19. Wilberforce, quoted in Wilberforce and Wilberforce, *Life*, 5:162;

Wilberforce, *A Practical View*, p. 47; Wilberforce, British Museum Add MSS 38191.280, Liverpool Papers, letter to Lord Liverpool, 30 Sep. 1821, cited by Pollock, p. 153.

20. Wilberforce, Diary, Sept. 17, 1830, cited by Furneaux, *Wilberforce*, p. 278.

21. Ervine, pp. 32-35.

22. Wilberforce, quoted in Wilberforce and Wilberforce, *Life*, 4:242.

23. Ibid.

24. Ibid., 2:165.

25. Ibid., 3:357, 4:246.

26. Ibid., 3:182.

27. Ibid., 3:303.

28. Ibid., 4:85.

29. Wilberforce, *A Practical View*, p. 307.

30. See Ervine, p. 279.

31. Ibid., p. 249.

32. Ibid.

33. Wilberforce, quoted in Wilberforce and Wilberforce, *Life*, 2:25

34. Ibid., 2:27.

35. Wilberforce, *A Practical View*, pp. 265-6.

36. Rosman, p. 13.

37. Wilberforce, *A Practical View*, p. 315.

38. Ibid., p. 317.

39. Ibid., p. 304.

40. Ibid., p. 296.

41. See Brown, p. 177.

42. *WDCS*, 1983 ed., s.v. "Puritan Spirituality," by N.H. Keeble.

43. Furneaux, *Wilberforce*, p. 41.

44. Coupland, p. 208.

45. Wilberforce, quoted in Wilberforce and Wilberforce, *Correspondence*, 1:50.

46. Ibid.

47. See Rosman, p. 72.

48. Wilberforce, quoted in Wilberforce and Wilberforce, *Life*, 4:260.

49. Ibid., 5:285.

50. Rosman, p. 75.

51. More, p. 60, cited ibid., p. 87.

52. Brown, p. 409.

53. Rosman, p. 89.

54. Wilberforce, quoted in Wilberforce and Wilberforce, *Life*, 4:389-90.

55. M.M. Knappen, ed., *Two Elizabethan Puritan Diaries* (Chicago: The American Society of Church History, 1933), p. 6.

56. More, quoted in W. Roberts, *Memoirs of the Life and Correspondence of Mrs. Hannah More*, vol. 2 (London, 1834), pp. 140-1, cited by Rosman, p. 120.

57. More, Duke MSS, Wilberforce Papers, letter to Wilberforce, n.d. (?1795), cited by Lean, p. 111.

58. Wilberforce, quoted in Wilberforce and Wilberforce, *Life*, 1:317.

59. Rosman, p. 119.

60. Wilberforce, *A Practical View*, p. 267.

61. Peter Lewis, *The Genius of Puritanism* (Haywards Heath: Carey Publications, 1975), p. 12.

62. *WDCS*, 1983 ed. s.v. "Puritan Spirituality," by N.H. Keeble.

63. Wilberforce, quoted in Wilberforce and Wilberforce, *Life*, 5:22

64. Ibid., 5:367.

65. Wilberforce, *A Practical View*, p. 268.

66. Wilberforce, quoted in Wilberforce and Wilberforce, *Life*, 4:248.

67. Wilberforce, *A Practical View*, pp. 185-6.

68. Wilberforce, quoted in Wilberforce and Wilberforce, *Life*, 5:93.

69. See Haller, p. 108, Simeon Ashe writing about Jeremiah Whitaker; Knappen, p. 66, Richard Rogers writing about a friend.

70. Wilberforce, quoted in Wilberforce and Wilberforce, *Life*, 4:166.

71. Ibid., 4:152.

72. Ibid., 4:310.

73. Rosman, p. 112.

74. Ibid., p. 114.

75. Wilberforce, quoted in Wilberforce and Wilberforce, *Life*, 3:310

76. Ibid., 4:248.

77. Ibid., 4:276.

78. Ibid., 5:161.

79. Wilberforce, quoted in Wilberforce and Wilberforce, *Correspondence*, 1:44.

80. Ibid., 1:45.

81. Ibid.

82. Ibid., 1:25.

83. Ibid., 1:27.

84. Ibid., 2:25.

85. Ibid., 2:26.

86. Ibid., 1:101.

87. Ibid., 1:26, 27.

88. Ibid., 2:173.

89. Ibid., 1:27.

90. Ibid., 2:192.

91. Furneaux, *Wilberforce*, p. 350.

92. See Wilberforce and Wilberforce, *Life*, 2:405.

93. Wilberforce, quoted in Jay, pp. 298-9.

94. Wilberforce, Sidmouth MSS, letter to Henry Addington, 9 Nov. 1799, cited by Pollock, p. 153.

95. Jay, p. 298.

96. Ibid., p. 305.

97. Wilberforce, Private Papers, pp. 275-6, cited by Furneaux, *Wilberforce*, p. 321.

98. Wilberforce, quoted in Wilberforce and Wilberforce, *Life*, 3:407.

99. Wilberforce, Hull MSS, Diary, n.d., cited by Pollock, p. 153.

100. Wilberforce, *A Practical View*, p. 267.

CHAPTER V

Friends

Major Influences on Wilberforce's Spirituality and Theology

It was John Donne, Anglican poet and pastor of the 17th century, who declared in his Meditation 17, that "no man is an island, entire of itself." This is particularly true of William Wilberforce. Wilberforce was a passionate and influential leader who transformed the times he lived in. But he was only able to do this because of the support and encouragement of many friends, some of whom were his contemporaries, some of whom he knew only through their books. Friendship was an important and integral aspect of Wilberforce's spirituality and life.

Isaac Milner

The Rev. Isaac Milner was one of Wilberforce's closest friends and he had a strong influence on the dynamic Evangelical leader. In 1829, nine years after Milner's death, Wilberforce wrote that he had based his religious principles on "perusal of the Holy Scriptures and ...the instruction I derived from a friend of very extraordinary natural and acquired powers."[1] Milner was instrumental, by his use of Philip Doddridge's book and the Greek New Testament, in helping lay

Wilberforce's spiritual and theological foundations.

One year after the coach ride during which Wilberforce was gradually converted to an Evangelical faith Milner received his Bachelor of Divinity degree from Cambridge. Two years after that, in 1788, he was appointed President of Queen's College, Cambridge and he set about making it an Evangelical stronghold.[2] Evangelical parents sent their sons to Queen's and young Evangelicals seeking ordination went there as well so that Queen's became one of the largest colleges in the University.[3] Appointed Dean of Carlisle in 1791, he spent his summers preaching at the cathedral in Carlisle (where he drew large crowds) and the rest of the year at Cambridge.

Milner was a man full of happiness and good cheer so he and Wilberforce always got along well. The only time they almost quarreled was over the question of Catholic Emancipation. Throughout Milner's life the two were in constant correspondence with each other and Milner opened himself up to Wilberforce as he did with no one else.[4] He encouraged Wilberforce during the struggle for Abolition of the slave trade: "If you carry this point in your whole life, that life will be far better spent than in being Prime Minister many years."[5] He may also have saved Wilberforce's life in 1796 when the young politician fell dangerously ill after losing a Third Reading of the Abolition Bill by four votes. "He was the means," wrote Wilberforce after his recovery, "if not of saving my life, at least of sparing me a long and dangerous fit of sickness in the last spring…When he is at an uncomeatable distance I never have the same sense of security."[6] Indeed, the two men made a point of getting together as often as possible, so that the influence Milner exerted on him extended well beyond the time of Wilberforce's conversion. "You might squeeze and tap him all day long," Wilberforce wrote in 1800, fifteen years after Milner had led him into an Evangelical faith, "and still you would find fresh supplies ready to be drawn off."[7]

John Newton

John Newton must stand as one of the strongest influences in Wilberforce's life. He was the first Evangelical preacher Wilberforce ever heard and he was the man whose words of counsel were constantly able to comfort Wilberforce during the difficult months following his conversion. Moreover, it was he (along with Pitt) who encouraged Wilberforce to stay in politics.

It is odd that Brown should say that Newton looked askance at Christians in politics.[8] As early as 1786 Newton had written of Wilberforce: "I hope the Lord will make him a blessing both as a Christian and a statesman. How seldom do these characters coincide!! But they are not incompatible."[9] He reinforced this sentiment over the years; in1788: "It is hoped and believed that the Lord has raised you up for the good of His church, and for the good of the nation";[10] and in 1796:

> I believe you are the Lord's servant, and are in the post which He has assigned you; and though it appears to me more arduous, and requiring more self-denial than my own, I know that He who has called you to it can afford you strength according to your day.[11]

"The old African blasphemer," as Newton liked to call himself, continued to befriend, encourage, and correspond with Wilberforce throughout his life, writing at least as late as June, 1804,[12] two months before his eightieth birthday and three years before his death on December 21, 1807. The two frequently breakfasted together and Wilberforce often went to hear Newton preach. They would have had no trouble getting along. William Jay said about Newton:

> There was nothing about him dull, or gloomy, or puritanical, according to the common meaning of the term. As he had much good-nature, so he had much pleasantry, and frequently emitted sparks of lively wit, or rather humor.[13]

Newton was a Calvinist, but as Brown puts it, "the possibly unique Calvinist to whom it made no difference whether a man called himself a Calvinist or not provided he was manifestly making his way to the Cross."[14] He was one of those who coaxed Wilberforce along the path of religious toleration and Evangelical ecumenism. "I am sick of the spirit of party of all parties," he once wrote. "I wish to be able to throw some water upon the fire of contention."[15] He also influenced Wilberforce concerning the reality of providence in which he was a great believer.[16]

It is difficult to say how much Newton affected Wilberforce in his attitude towards slavery. It is doubtful that he was outspoken against it when Wilberforce heard him as a boy. Yet Wilberforce may well have picked up something at this point—Newton had already published his autobiography four years before Wilberforce came to live with his Methodist uncle and aunt, and in it he expressed some doubt about the morality of the slave trade. As his thoughts against slavery congealed, some of this thinking may have come out in the sermons Wilberforce heard. Newton was also in contact with John Wesley who published an anti-slavery pamphlet in 1774. In 1780, when Newton came to St. Mary Woolnoth in London, he was criticizing slavery openly,[17] and by 1787 he had published at least one condemnation of it.[18] It is certain that the young convert of 1785 heard Newton's ugly stories about the slave trade and was encouraged by him to take his stand against it in Parliament.[19]

Philip Doddridge

Philip Doddridge, the English Nonconformist minister, was born in 1702 and died eight years before Wilberforce's birth. Yet of any single person he had the greatest influence on Wilberforce's life. This came about through his writings, principally his book *The Rise and Progress of Religion in the Soul* published in 1745. This was the book which, along with the Greek New Testament and Isaac Milner's instruction, brought Wilberforce to Christ and to an Evangelical faith. Wilberforce never grew tired of the volume. In 1797 it was still "that most useful book,"[20] and in 1803 he gave it to a young convict who was soon after executed for forgery—"We trust it has pleased God to bless the means which we have used, and that the poor man is a true convert."[21] Wilberforce read a great deal of Doddridge: his biography, his published letters, two volumes of his sermons (the one on the theme of regeneration and the other on the power and grace of Christ).[22] But the parallels between *The Rise and Progress* and Wilberforce's own writing and thinking remain the most remarkable.

The book begins with Doddridge's condemnation of national sin written in much the same tone and language as Wilberforce would use to attack England's sin in his *Practical View*. Doddridge uses the term "vital Christianity" to describe true Christianity as opposed to nominalism, a term which Wilberforce would pick up and use also.[23] Doddridge is strong on sin, judgment, hell, salvation by grace, and the substitutionary atonement, as Wilberforce would be.[24] He emphasizes that some of the critical elements of a Christian lifestyle are spiritual mindedness, obedience, faith in and love to Christ, joy in Christ, and humility, just as Wilberforce would do.[25] He speaks of the importance of daily self-examination,[26] prayer,[27] and of the Lord's Supper (Eucharist).[28] He talks of the critical importance of maintaining continual communion with God, the heart of Wilberforce's spirituality.[29] He stresses early morning devotions, diligence in business, prudence in recreation, the careful observation of providence, the importance of solitude.[30] He teaches the devotional, as opposed to the critical, reading of the Bible.[31] He teaches the use of the Psalms,[32] the importance of evening devotions,[33] the place of repentance, praise and petition,[34] the value of time,[35] the certainty and importance of death and judgment, of rejoicing in this fact and dying well.[36] He also teaches the need to develop an expectancy of heaven,[37] the resistance of specific temptations,[38] that great afflictions come from God's right hand and ought to be borne with patience and thankfulness, as well as inquired into and complied with when the reasons for them are understood.[39] He admonishes benevolence to humankind and usefulness.[40] In short, everything that Doddridge points up will become part of the fabric of Wilberforce's theology and spirituality. From the very beginning Wilberforce "resolved to practise Doddridge's rules," praying to God to enable him.[41] The spiritual disciplines which were fostered in Wilberforce through Doddridge's book never lost their grip.

When Wilberforce partook of Doddridge and his teachings he was partaking of Puritanism. "It is," states A.T.S. James, "the early Puritan mysticism, no doubt modified and reduced, but the same in its faith and its spiritual perceptiveness."[42] There was a good reason for this.

Doddridge's favourite theologian was Richard Baxter. "Baxter is my particular favourite," he wrote, "and it is impossible to tell you how much I am charmed with the education, good sense, and pathos, which are everywhere to be found in that writer."[43] Doddridge was, according to Gordon S. Wakefield, "a Dissenting Divine in the succession of Richard Baxter and John Howe."[44] What he shared with and gained from Baxter included a concern for Christian unity, a practical faith, and a strong vision of heaven (to name a few). These he passed on to Wilberforce in his writings. He, like Newton, moved Wilberforce toward a position of religious toleration. "He was," says Geoffrey Nuttall of Doddridge, "desirous in principle not to exclude any whose theology might be mistaken but whose devotion to Jesus Christ, for all that, was unmistakable."[45] Wilberforce, as in so many areas, followed Doddridge's example here.

Doddridge was to Wilberforce "a wonderful man,"[46] and it was to him Wilberforce owed the backbone of his religious development. Unquestionably it was Doddridge who led Wilberforce to Baxter's *Practical Works* which were as influential in the young politician's life and spirituality as they had been in Doddridge's—Baxter's *Self Review* was the blueprint for Doddridge's *The Rise and Progress of Religion in the Soul*.[47]

Richard Baxter

Richard Baxter (1615-1691), was an English Puritan minister who withdrew from the Church of England in 1662 to take on the leadership of the moderate or Presbyterian Nonconformists. His particular brand of spirituality became known as Baxterianism—a practical spirituality that had no place for controversial or speculative theology. It was also a spirituality which emphasized only the most crucial aspects of Christianity, the few fundamentals on which the variety of Christian denominations might be able to reach a consensus. The "mere Christian" was a person who would hold to the Decalogue, the Apostle's Creed, and the Lord's Prayer "by a faith that worketh by love."[48] "Provided there be this faith," Baxter said, "it matters not what opinions a man holds on any theological or ecclesiastical question, nor whether he be in error in these incidentals."[49] Horton Davies has called Baxter "the first exponent of Ecumenism in England."[50]

Wilberforce had already been reading a lot of Baxter by the time he wrote *A Practical View*: "I must...express my unfeigned and high respect for this great man...his practical writings, in four great massy [sic] volumes, are a treasury of Christian wisdom."[51] These four quarto volumes were constantly at his side, as much in 1814—"Having a cold I staid at home and read Baxter. Much pleased, and I hope edified."[52]—as in his years of retirement, when they remained a good companion.[53] He was all for seeing the four large volumes revised and abridged for modern readers. Baxter's "*Life* also, written by himself," Wilberforce said, "contains much useful matter."[54]

Baxter was not only "useful" for Wilberforce in terms of encouraging a tolerance for other Christian groups. His concerns for a "practical religion" exactly coincided with Wilberforce's temperament. Baxter wrote *The Christian Directory* in order to help a person bring Christianity and their career together. He also spoke about the importance of social justice.[55] As early as 1673 he condemned the slave trade as "one of the worst kinds of Thievery in the world" and said slave owners were "fitter to be called incarnate Devils than Christians."[56]

There were other points of emphasis in Baxter which can be seen in Wilberforce as well. Baxter spoke out on the importance of Sunday as the Lord's Day.[57] Solitude was important to him: "I would advise thee to frequent solitariness, that thou mayest sometimes confer with Christ and with they self."[58] Joy was important: "The life of Christ is a life of joy."[59] His treatises such as *The Saints' Everlasting Rest* and *Dying Thoughts* stressed the role in the Christian's life of meditation, of contemplation of heaven, of being ready to die and be with God. "Bend thy soul," he wrote, "to study eternity, busie it about the life to come, habituate thy self to such contemplations...bathe thy soul in heavens [sic] Delights."[60] He emphasized the need for self-examination in order to see and remember God's providential workings.[61] He appreciated nature as an aid to the contemplation of heaven,[62] as well as to observing the goodness of God.[63] His goal was to do everything to the glory of God.[64] Each of these aspects of his spirituality was important to Wilberforce. Baxter's *Practical Works* was a constant reinforcement to Wilberforce's religious exercises.

It is probable that Wilberforce also found some help in Baxter's struggle with poor physical health and the suffering that accompanied it. Often close to death due to his many illnesses, Baxter wrote a friend, "Weakness and pain helped me to study how to die, that set me on studying how to live."[65] What he came to understand about spirituality and God from his physical handicaps enabled him to become a very active man, having learned the secret of gaining new strength from mediation and prayer.[66] Plagued by a weak physical constitution himself, yet able to achieve in his lifetime far beyond what many healthy persons might accomplish, Wilberforce appears to have learnt about prayer and meditation what his mentor Baxter did and applied it to the same effect.

John Owen

Sin and the personal struggle against it were strong realities in Wilberforce's life. It is not surprising then that he involved himself in the spiritual discipline of mortification. Mortification is the act of "putting to death" one's sins, weakening them to such a degree that they are no longer effective in manipulating the believer's will. Since this was an area of particular expertise and pastoral concern for the Puritan Nonconformist John Owen, it is not surprising that Wilberforce spent a good amount of time in the man's writings.

John Owen (1616-1683), is considered one of the greatest of the Puritan divines or theologians. Wilberforce was reading him at least as early as 1791, six years after his conversion.[67] In *A Practical View* he recommends two of Owen's treatises: *The Grace and Duty of Being Spirituality Minded* and *Of the Mortification of Sin in Believers*.[68] The first aided Wilberforce in his endeavours to be constantly mindful of Christ and of the reality of heaven. "Possess your minds," wrote Owen, "with right notions and apprehensions of things above, and of the state of future glory."[69] It also helped reinforce other related aspects of Puritan contemplation.

Owen teaches that the dispensations of providence,[70] special trials and temptations,[71] heavenly and eternal realities,[72] all these should be the objects of a believer's spiritual thoughts. The grand object ought to be "God in Christ."[73] The Christian needs to pray,[74] to use Scripture in meditation,[75] to mortify sin and beware of useless thoughts,[76] all in order to enjoy having Christ continually on the mind.[77] These are constant subjects in Wilberforce's journals and diaries. No wonder he found the treatise "eminently useful"[78] and was still referring to it directly in 1812.[79]

The second treatise was equally influential for Wilberforce. Two important elements in Owen's approach to mortification—the concentration on the sin nature instead of individual sins, as well as the belief that it is ultimately God through the Holy Spirit who mortifies sin[80]—appear as early as 1789 in Wilberforce's diary:

> My error hitherto has been, I think, endeavouring to amend this
> and the other failing, instead of striking at the root of evil. Let
> me therefore make a spirited effort, not trusting in myself, but
> in the strength of the Lord God.[81]

At the end of the year he writes of the importance of "mortifying the flesh…let it be my main care to exterminate a sensual spirit rather by substituting better regards in its place, than by attacking it directly."[82] This was yet another element in Owen's approach to mortification— sin was best overcome not simply by struggling to root it out but by developing the fruit of the Spirit to such an extent that sin would be crowded out.[83]

The summer of 1790 finds Wilberforce carrying on in much the same vein: "Oh may I from this time cultivate heavenly affections by mortifying the flesh, and living much in the view of unseen things, and may the Spirit of the Lord sanctify me wholly."[84] He finally mentions Owen by name in the summer of 1792 and that he has been reading him.[85] In 1810 he is aware of a problem Owen has pointed out, "a trade of sinning and repenting,"[86] a vicious circle of not really trying to stop habitual sins from recurring that he is afraid he is getting caught up in.

Owen was a theologian whose treatises Wilberforce obviously spent some time on, so that portions of it became committed to memory. References in his diaries and journals to specific items of Owen's teaching are frequent.[87]

John Venn

The Clapham Group existed from 1792 until 1815 and it consisted of people like Henry Thornton, a banker and the son of John Thornton; Thomas Babington, a landed magnate; James Stephen, a lawyer; Zachary Macaulay, the editor of *The Christian Observer*; Lord Teignmouth, formerly the Governor-General of India; Hannah More, the novelist. Most of the persons involved were Anglicans and supporters of the Tory government, but at least one was a Nonconformist and another a member of the Opposition in the House of Commons.[88] The individual among them who exerted perhaps the most influence on Wilberforce was John Venn, son of the famous preacher Henry Venn. John Venn, an Evangelical, became the minister of the Clapham parish in 1793. Until his death in 1813 he was "the fellow conspirator, the personal friend, and the spiritual guide of the Clapham brotherhood."[89]

Wilberforce reveled under Venn's teaching. When Venn first arrived at Clapham he "preached an excellent introductory sermon."[90] From that point on, Wilberforce encouraged others to open their pulpits to him when Venn was traveling,[91] invited those who did not know Christ to come and hear Venn preach,[92] and lent out copies of Venn's sermons.[93] He was the "heavenly-minded" Venn, "bent on his Master's work, affectionate to all around him, and above all to Christ's people…Oh let me labour with redoubled diligence, to enter in at the strait gate."[94]

Wilberforce was not blind to Venn's failings—"we discussed and told Venn his faults"—but appreciated the breadth and the depth of his Evangelical preaching.[95] Venn was criticized by others because he did not always preach evangelistic messages from key texts, but looked for significance in all of Scripture. This helped Wilberforce's spiritual growth: "He [Venn] acknowledged, and we too, who much agree with him, that he does not agree with any of the gospel preachers. They swell one part to the lessening of another; strain and pervert

Scripture."[96] Venn also contributed to Wilberforce's adoption of a stance of religious toleration.[97]

Despite his critics, Venn was a popular preacher. His congregations were large. Extremely fond of Venn, Wilberforce hoped Pitt would make him a bishop so that his godly influence could be more widespread.[98] Wilberforce may even have expressed this hope to his old friend and Prime Minister. But Pitt did not do so.

Others

There were many others who made an impact on Wilberforce's spirituality and theology to a greater or lesser extent through their books, their preaching, or through personal contact. Baxter and Owen, for example, were not the only Puritans Wilberforce read. He thought highly of John Flavel and John Howe, both seventeenth century Puritans.[99] Howe had been a Presbyterian minister who emphasized religious tolerance. He had stressed contemplation of God, enjoyment of God, and being prepared for heaven as incentives to holiness: "Read Howe *On Delighting in God*, and much affected by it."[100] Wilberforce also read the American Puritan Jonathan Edwards, who died the year before Wilberforce's birth.[101]

Wilberforce enjoyed Anglican writers like George Herbert (1593-1633), the clergyman-poet who had such a strong influence on Richard Baxter;[102] Thomas Hooker, whom he considered "excellent;"[103] and Bishop Joseph Butler, who died in 1752 and whose *Analogy of Religion*, published in 1736, was recommended by Pitt, read by Wilberforce in 1785,[104] and mentioned favourably in his private papers.[105] Basically, Butler argued that as humans were governed by a supreme conscience, so nature was governed by a moral being that was revealed through this conscience. Humans lived, in fact, under the government of this moral being, a government that encouraged virtue and discouraged vice. From this stance, Butler argued for a future life where justice would prevail, discussed the problem of free will and determinism, and attempted to draw a line from the moral governor and the world's moral climate to the doctrines of the Christian revelation.[106]

Wilberforce read Blaise Pascal early on when he was converted and continued to spend time in his writings. Pascal, who died in 1662, wrote the classic *Pensées, Thoughts on Religion*, which Wilberforce found "highly valuable, though not in every part to be approved."[107] *Pensées* consisted of fragments of a planned apologia for the Christian faith which was published posthumously in 1670. It is not hard to surmise which elements of Pascal's thought Wilberforce would have found most attractive. Pascal emphasized that humans were alienated without God, that the Fall had occurred, that Redemption had been accomplished, that it was important to find God through the heart rather than the intellect.[108] He stressed the concrete ways in which Christian commitment can improve the situation of others.[109] What binds all of Pascal's "thoughts" together is a strong and consistent Christocentricity.[110]

He was also helped by another Frenchman, Francois Fénelon (1651-1715), who had been heavily affected by the teachings of Madame Guyon. The translations of A. M. Ramsay made Fénelon popular in England in the 1700's. Fénelon's stress on the development of the spiritual life and on the disinterested love of God won him many Protestant admirers. Wilberforce read and remembered his advice.[111]

Wilberforce was aided by the Rev. John Witherspoon (1723-1794), a Presbyterian theologian and a statesman. Witherspoon had made something of a name for himself in 1756 when a book he had written on justification and holiness was published, "one of the ablest expositions of the Calvinist doctrine in any language."[112] Wilberforce even wrote a preface to Witherspoon's *Essay on Regeneration* which had been of great practical help to him.[113]

Wilberforce enjoyed the poetry and the hymns of William Cowper (1731-1800), the good friend of John Newton,[114] as well as the verse and friendship of the poet Robert Southey.[115] Personal friendships with evangelical clergymen were also important. He wrote long letters to the Rev. Dr. Thomas Chalmers, a leading figure in the Church of Scotland, whom he considered "truly pious, simple, and unassuming."[116] He heard him preach when Chalmers was in London in 1817 and found some of the sermons to his taste, others not.[117] But he loved Chalmers, whose friendship he told Chalmers he coveted,[118] and Chalmers, who had been profoundly influenced by *A Practical View*, returned the affection, writing Wilberforce in 1828:

> May you still have many days of rest, and of rejoicing on the borders of heaven. And may that book which spoke powerfully to myself, and has spoken powerfully to thousands, represent you to future generations, and be the instrument of converting many who are yet unborn.[119]

Another Evangelical clergyman whose friendship was important to Wilberforce was Charles Simeon who was a Fellow of King's College, Cambridge and became the minister of Trinity Church in 1783. Simeon was the great clerical leader of the Evangelical Movement. Wilberforce often wrote him letters where he addressed Simeon as "my dear friend."[120] Simeon was a strong inspiration to Wilberforce, who wrote in his diary in 1797: "Simeon with us—his heart glowing with love of Christ. How full he is of love, and of desire to promote the spiritual benefit of others. Oh that I might copy him, as he Christ."[121]

There were other clergymen who influenced Wilberforce, such as the Calvinist Thomas Scott and the Nonconformist William Jay Scott had an impact on Wilberforce from the very beginning,[122] and Wilberforce considered Scott the best preacher he had ever heard, at least up until the time he sat under the preaching of John Venn.[123] William Jay was the minister in whose presence Wilberforce, on his deathbed, confirmed that he continued to hold to his Evangelical beliefs. The two corresponded and frequently met together throughout Wilberforce's life. Wilberforce read and was helped by two volumes of Jay's sermons and was very pleased when the Dissenting minister dedicated his volume of spiritual meditations, entitled *Evening Exercises*, to Wilberforce.[124]

Wilberforce wrote Jay in the spring of 1826:

> Both you and I, I believe, and indeed I cannot doubt it, are much more closely bound to each other by the substance of Christian principles,...then we are separated by any differences as to the outward form and mechanism of religion.[125]

When one scans the various persons and books which contributed to Wilberforce's spirituality it is not difficult to discern from which quarters the greatest influence came. First of all, one realizes the preponderance of Calvinists in his spiritual lineage: Newton, Owen, Howe, Edwards, Witherspoon, Scott, to name a few. Clearly, it was the cold and intellectual Calvinism, even hyper-Calvinism, with which he found fault. A warm and practical Calvinism of the heart he obviously relished and learned a great deal from. Secondly, one distinguishes the decided Puritan influence: Doddridge, Baxter, Owen, Flavel, Howe, Edwards. It is small wonder then if Wilberforce's spirituality should manifest so many Puritan traits and encourage the author of this biography to term him a Puritan also (see Chapter IV). Thirdly, one sees the influence of Baxter's "mere Christianity" in Wilberforce's wide range of spiritual reading. He could benefit from a Dissenting Doddridge as well as from an Anglican Butler, a Catholic Pascal as well as from a Calvinistic Owen, from an evangelical Jay and a mystic like Fenelon both. Wherever he could find God and Christ, wherever he could find help in seeing and serving that God and Christ, there Wilberforce went. His spiritual tastes ran along the same lines as his spiritual service, namely that which honoured God and that which was eminently practical.

Notes

1. Wilberforce, St. John's, Cantab. MSS, letter to Sir Edward Parry, 25 June 1829, cited by Pollock, p. 35.

2. *DNB*, 1949-50 ed., s.v. "Isaac Milner."

3. *Ibid.*

4. *Ibid.* One example is a letter to Wilberforce in which Milner admits his desire for the mastership of Trinity College.

5. Milner, Bodleian Library, c.3.35, letter to Wilberforce, 1793, cited by Pollock, p. 87.

6. Wilberforce, Stanhope MSS 731(12), letter to George Pretyman, bishop of Lincoln, 30 June 1796, cited by Pollock, p. 144.

7. Wilberforce, Huntington MSS, Montagu Papers, letter to Matthew Montagu, 14 October 1800, cited by Pollock, p. 145.

8. Brown, p. 132.

9. John Newton, letter to William Cowper, 1786, cited by Pollock, *Amazing Grace* (San Francisco: Harper & Row, 1981), p. 175.

10. Newton, quoted in Wilberforce and Wilberforce, *Correspondence*, 1:56.

11. *Ibid.*, 1:130-1.

12. *Ibid.*, 1:302.

13. Jay, p. 270.

14. Brown, p. 172.

15. Newton, Olney MSS, cited by Pollock, *Grace*, p. 161.

16. See Josiah Bull, *John Newton*, (London: The Religious Tract Society, 1868), p. 367; Newton, *The Life of the Rev. John Newton*, (London: The Religious Tract Society, n.d.), p. 106.

17. Pollock, *Grace*, p. 173.

18. Brown, p. 106.

19. The first authenticated account of Wilberforce's interest in the slave trade appears to be a statement made in 1780 to one of the Members for Hull, David Hartley. In 1776 Hartley had introduced a motion designed to lay the way for abolition. Wilberforce recalled: "I expressed my hope to him [Hartley] that the time would come when I should be able to do something on behalf of the slaves." See Pollock, *Wilberforce*, p. 11.

20. Wilberforce, *A Practical View*, p. 297.

21. Wilberforce, quoted in Wilberforce and Wilberforce, *Life*, 3:83.

22. See Wilberforce, *A Practical View*, p. 297; also Wilberforce, quoted in Wilberforce and Wilberforce, Life, 1:232, 319.

23. Doddridge, p. 149; cf. Wilberforce, *A Practical View*, p. 315.

24. Doddridge, p. 214.

25. Ibid., p. 268.

26. Ibid., pp. 280, 316.

27. Ibid., p. 284.

28. Ibid., p. 308.

29. *Ibid.*, p. 316.

30. *Ibid.*

31. *Ibid.*, p. 320.

32. *Ibid.*, p. 321.

33. *Ibid.*, p. 326.

34. *Ibid.*, p. 327-8.

35. *Ibid.*, p. 325.

36. *Ibid.*, pp. 325, 431, 439.

37. *Ibid.*, p. 328.

38. *Ibid.*, p. 343.

39. *Ibid.*, p. 389.

40. *Ibid.*, p. 417.

41. Wilberforce, quoted in Wilberforce and Wilberforce, *Life*, 1:102.

42. James, "Doddridge: His Influence," in Nuttall, ed., *Doddridge*, p. 37.

43. Doddridge, *Correspondence and Diary of Philip Doddridge*, ed. J.D. Humphreys (London, n.d.), cited by Nuttall, *Richard Baxter and Philip Doddridge* (London: Oxford University Press, 1951), p. 18.

44. *WDCS*, 1983 ed., s.v. "Philip Doddridge," by Gordon S. Wakefield.

45. Nuttall, *Doddridge*, p. 15.

46. Wilberforce, quoted in Wilberforce and Wilberforce, *Life*, 1:319.

47. James, in Nuttall, *Doddridge*, p. 36.

48. Richard Baxter, *Naked Popery* (London, 1677), p. 7; *The True Catholik and Catholik Church Described* (London, 1660), pp. 10, 16-17, 19; *Universal Concord* (London, 1660), p. 33; cited by N.H. Keeble, *Richard Baxter* (Oxford: Clarendon Press, 1982), p. 24.

49. *Ibid.*

50. Horton Davies, *The English Free Churches* (London: Home University library, n.d.), p. 79, Hugh Martin, *Puritanism and Richard Baxter* (London: SCM Press Ltd., 1954), p. 158.

51. Wilberforce, *A Practical View*, p. 295.

52. Wilberforce, quoted in Wilberforce and Wilberforce, *Life*, 4:163.

53. Ibid., 5:249; Coupland, p. 188.

54. Wilberforce, *A Practical View*, p. 295.

55. Martin, p. 171.

56. Baxter, *A Christian Directory*, Vol. 4 (London, 1673), pp. 557ff., cited by Martin, pp. 174-5.

57. See Martin, p. 107.

58. Baxter, *The Saints' Everlasting Rest* (London, 1650), pp. 713, 703, cited by Keeble, p. 103.

59. Baxter, ibid., pp. 600-1, cited ibid., p. 94.

60. Ibid.

61. Baxter, *The Mischiefs of Self-Ignorance and the Benefits of Self-Acquaintance* (London, 1662), p. 185, cited by ibid., pp. 133, 143.

62. See Keeble, ibid., p. 95.

63. Baxter, *The Reasons of the Christian Religion* (London, 1667), p. 108, cited by Frederick J. Powicke, *The Rev. Richard Baxter Under the Cross* (London: Jonathan Cape Ltd., 1927), p. 243.

64. See Powicke, p. 259.

65. Baxter, *The Autobiography of Richard Baxter*, ed. J.M. Lloyd Thomas (reprint ed., London: J.M. Dent & Sons Ltd., 1931), p. xvii.

66. Baxter was curate at Kidderminster from 1641-61, and authored ten books and 131 other pieces, including a large number of unpublished treatises in his lifetime (five of the books were published posthumously). See J.I. Packer, Foreward to Baxter, *The Reformed Pastor*, ed. William Brown (1656; repr. ed., Edinburgh: The Banner of Truth Trust, 1974), p. 9. It is interesting to note that Baxter taught that Christ's death had brought about a universal redemption on the basis of which God had made a new law. Repentance and faith in this universal redemption were obedience to this law and resulted in God's forgiveness. Thus the believer's personal saving righteousness was tied less into Christ's redemption than the repentance and faith which constituted obedience to the new law the redemption had, in fact, established. The works-righteousness implicit in this soteriological scheme created a highly moralistic Unitarianism which Wilberforce briefly flirted with. However, in the end,

Wilberforce fought this sort of scheme in *A Practical View*. There he insisted that "real Christianity" started with a believer whose only claim to saving righteousness was Christ's redemption, period, not his or her's faith and repentance. Wilberforce was attracted by Baxter's pastoral writings, not his controversial doctrinal ones, as was the case with the majority of the religious writers he read. See Packer, ibid., p. 10.

67. Wilberforce, quoted in Wilberforce and Wilberforce, *Life*, 1:312.

68. Wilberforce, *A Practical View*, p. 296.

69. John Owen, *The Works of John Owen*, ed. William H. Goold, vol. 7; *The Grace and Duty of Being Spiritually Minded* (New York: Robert Carter and Brothers, 1852), p. 332.

70. Ibid., p. 308.

71. Ibid., p. 312.

72. Ibid., p. 317.

73. Ibid., p. 337.

74. Ibid., pp. 287ff.

75. Ibid., p. 347.

76. Ibid., pp. 407, 304.

77. Ibid., p. 346.

78. Wilberforce, Diary, Sept. 17, 1830, cited by Furneaux, *Wilberforce*, p. 278.

79. Wilberforce, quoted in Wilberforce and Wilberforce, *Life*, 4:82.

80. Owen, vol. 6: *Of the Mortification of Sin in Believers*, p. 40; Owen, *The Holy Spirit: His gifts and power* (reprint ed., Grand Rapids: Kregel Publications, 1954), p. 312.

81. Wilberforce, quoted in Wilberforce and Wilberforce, *Life*, 1:207.

82. Ibid., 1:250-1.

83. Owen, *The Holy Spirit*, p. 312.

84. Wilberforce, quoted in Wilberforce and Wilberforce, *Life*, 1:275.

85. Ibid., 1:363.

86. Ibid., 3:437.

87. See Wilberforce, quoted in Wilberforce and Wilberforce, *Life*,

1:207, 250, 251, 253, 275, 363; 3:437; 4:82.

88. Elie Halevy, *A History of the English People in 1815* (New York: Harcourt, Brace & Co., 1924), p. 381.

89. Howse, p. 16.

90. Wilberforce, quoted in Wilberforce and Wilberforce, Life, 2:16.

91. *Ibid.*, 2:31.

92. *Ibid.*, 2:405.

93. *Ibid.*

94. *Ibid.*, 2:32.

95. *Ibid.*, 2:136.

96. *Ibid.*, 2:136-7.

97. See Bloesch, 2:265.

98. Pollock, *Wilberforce*, p. 118.

99. Wilberforce, *A Practical View*, p. 296; Wilberforce, quoted in Wilberforce and Wilberforce, *Life*, 5:190.

100. Wilberforce, quoted in Wilberforce and Wilberforce, *Life*, 1:360.

101. *Ibid.*, 1:312.

102. Furneaux, Foreward to Wilberforce, *Journey*, p. 87.

103. Wilberforce, *A Practical View*, p. 30; cf. Wilberforce, quoted in Wilberforce and Wilberforce, *Life*, 4:318.

104. Wilberforce, quoted in Wilberforce and Wilberforce, *Life*, 1:90-1.

105. *Ibid.*, 4:274.

106. See *DNB*, 1949-50 ed., s.v. "Joseph Butler."

107. Wilberforce, *A Practical View*, pp. 375, 264.

108. *WDCS*, 1983 ed., s.v. "Blaise Pascal," by A.J. Krailsheimer.

109. *Ibid.*

110. *Ibid.*

111. Wilberforce, quoted in Wilberforce and Wilberforce, *Life*, 5:308.

112. *DNB*, 1949-50 ed., s.v. "John Witherspoon."

113. Wilberforce and Wilberforce, *Life*, 5:161.

114. Wilberforce, quoted ibid., 3:191.

115. Ibid., 5:29.

116. Ibid., 4:324.

117. Ibid.

118. Ibid., 5:29.

119. Thomas Chalmers, quoted in Wilberforce and Wilberforce, *Life*, 5:294.

120. Wilberforce, quoted in ibid., 3:354 and 5:14.

121. Ibid., 2:226.

122. Wilberforce, quoted in Wilberforce and Wilberforce, *Life*, 4:44.

123. See Pollock, p. 66.

124. See Jay, pp. 300 and 306.

125. Wilberforce, quoted in Jay, pp. 303-4.

CHAPTER VI

Vital Christianity
The Impact on Wilberforce and his Generation

Wilberforce's Evangelical faith not only had a pronounced impact on himself but also on Britain and the British Empire. As we have seen, Wilberforce's life took a decidedly different course after his conversion. His moral and ethical concerns were strengthened. He became increasingly a man of religious principle rather than party spirit. He became a disciplined man, not only in the way in which he approached his political workload, but as regards his personal habits as well— eating, sleeping, use of free time, the kind of books read, the sort of company kept. He learned to control his temper, his biting sarcasm, his love of human accolade, the fondness for overindulging in food and drink he shared with others of his social position and vocation. In one day he withdrew his membership from five fashionable London clubs. He gave up gambling. He gave up ballroom dancing. He gave up the theatre. He began to keep Sunday as a sacred day. When he took up his various causes, he took them up in God's name, not his own or his party's, and he saw them through not because it was politically expedient but because it was his belief that he ought to do so as a Christian called by God to persevere in the same. Yet, in due time, he would consider his family more important than his political career.

All of this stemmed from his conversion and the subsequent development of an Evangelical understanding of the Christian faith. The foregoing examination of Wilberforce's journals and diaries and correspondence has made this evident. Coupland concurs, stating that Wilberforce's conversion was "the supreme event" of his life, an event that never lost its hold on him but empowered his forty-eight remaining years:

> The capacity it had given him to meet the "blows of circum-stance" not merely with resignation but—in moments, at any rate, of solitude and contemplation—with serenity, had lost nothing of its power. We must understand this, indeed, if we would understand the man at all.[1]

Coupland goes on to state that Wilberforce's religious thought and concurrent spiritual disciplines became the backbone of his life and career:

> They did not enervate, they braced him, for the business of the active world outside. Whatever we may call it, it was not mor-bidity which enabled this chronic invalid to fight down fatigue, to work as hard, day in, day out, as most stronger men; to brush aside the worry of hostility and insult; to hold up, year after year, almost single-handed, the drooping banner of his cause; and finally to achieve as great a thing as any of his great contempo-raries achieved for the good name of his country and the welfare of mankind.[2]

On His Political Career

"At the beginning of 1785," states Furneaux, Wilberforce "had been an ambitious and able politician, whose time was divided between the advancement of his own career and the pursuit of pleasure." After his conversion, however, "for Wilberforce to remain in politics he had to use his position for something more than self-advancement. He had to make it a platform for his religious views and find causes that would wed his new beliefs with his old profession."[3]

The converted politician would discover many causes in which to serve his God and humankind. In only one of them, the opening of India to missionary activity, would his beliefs be explicitly aired in the House of Commons. Conscious that talking about religion too much would weaken his influence in the House, he guarded against it. Nevertheless, his religious beliefs were implicit in everything he did. Wilberforce felt that a politician must not be less sensitive to religion but more so. Religion was not only everyone's business, but "its advancement or decline in any country is so intimately connected with the temporal interests of society, as to render it the peculiar concern of a political man."[4]

All the causes Wilberforce undertook, all the debates he participated in, all the votes he cast, were all undergirded by prayer and Bible reading and his Christian conviction. The specific examples which may be cited are numerous. As his battle to bring an end to the British slave trade began to warm up, he wrote, "In truth, the principles upon which I act in this business being those of religion, not of sensibility and personal feeling, can know no remission, and yield to no delay."[5] When Pitt was angered at the revolt of the slaves in St. Domingo and the cause of Abolition was threatened, Wilberforce knew he must serve God despite the crisis: "I could hardly bring myself to resolve to do my duty and please God at the expense...of my cordiality with Pitt, or rather his with me."[6] In January of 1805, he anticipated the coming debate in the House when he should move the abolition of the slave trade once more:

> O Lord, do Thou fit me for it. Enable me to seek Thy glory, and not my own; to watch unto prayer; to wait diligently on God; to love Him and my Redeemer from the heart; and to be constrained by this love to live actively and faithfully devoting all my faculties and powers to His service, and the benefit of my fellow-creatures. Especially let me discharge with fidelity and humility the duties of my proper station, as unto the Lord, and not unto men;...O Lord, do Thou lead and guide me.[7]

When Abolition was defeated yet again, he nevertheless continued to pray that the slave trade might be ended:

O Lord, purify me. I do not, God be merciful to me, deserve the signal honour of being the instrument of putting an end to this atrocious and unparalleled wickedness. But, O Lord, let me earnestly pray Thee to pity these children of affliction, and to terminate their unequalled wrongs; and O direct and guide me in this important conjuncture, that I may act so as may be most agreeable to Thy will. Amen.[8]

His belief in a personal God and in the power of prayer to bring both himself and circumstances in line with the Divine will never flagged. He constantly asked God for guidance and believed in God's support. For example, regarding war with France: "I go to pray to Him, as I have often done, to direct me right in politics, and above all to renew my heart;"[9] when there was public uproar over his support of the Sedition Bills: "Let me look before me and solemnly implore the aid of God, to guide, quicken, and preserve me;"[10] for his many causes in the quiet of Good Friday: "Pray for my country both in temporal and spiritual things. Pray for political wisdom;...for the poor slaves; for the Abolition; for Sierra Leone;...Think over my enemies with forgiveness and love;"[11] when Henry Addington's Prime Ministership was on the line: "O Lord, to Thee I will pray, to enlighten my understanding and direct my judgment, and then to strengthen me to take the path of duty with a firm and composed though feeling mind;"[12] over resigning his influential Yorkshire seat: "I wished to devote to-day especially to the important purpose of seeking God's direction on the question, whether or not I should resign Yorkshire;"[13] regarding Catholic Emancipation: "Lord, direct me, all the religious people are on the other side, but they are sadly prejudiced...Blessed be God, they cannot be finally wrong in Thy sight who obey conscience, having taken due pains to inform themselves and judge rightly;"[14] when he was about to meet with the Russian Emperor Alexander to discuss General Abolition: "Got up by half-past six, that I might pray to God for a blessing on my interview;"[15] before speaking out in favor of the Corn Bill: "At my prayers this morning...I reflected seriously if it was not my duty to declare my opinions in favour of the Corn Bill, on the principle of providing things honest in the sight of all men, and adorning the doctrine of God my Saviour in all things. I decided to do it;"[16] in the controversy over registering slaves in order to be sure no more were being smuggled into the West Indies after the Abolition of 1807: "Our cause is good, and let us not fear; assuredly God will ultimately vindicate the side of justice and mercy;"[17] with the necessity of a decision on the Arms Seizing Bill: "O Lord, enable me to decide aright. Blessed by God, I serve a Master who takes the will for the deed;"[18] on the issue of George IV attempting to divorce Queen Caroline: "Pray for me, that I may be enlightened and strengthened for the duties of this important and critical season. Hitherto God has wonderfully supported and blessed me; oh how much beyond my deserts!"[19]

Wilberforce was frequently ridiculed for ambivalence. The truth was, a political independent and a man with a strong sense of his responsibility before God, to say nothing of country, he wrestled a great deal when it came time to choose sides in a debate. "The indecisiveness," says Pollock, "sprang from his honesty, his anxiety to do right by the nation and God at every twist of the political road in troublous times."[20] James Stephen, one of the Clapham Group, had a young son who later commented about this in his *Anti-Slavery Recollections*:

> Men might doubt about his vote on minor issues, but where the interests of morality, or humanity, or religion were involved, there Wilberforce's perception of what was right appeared intuitive, and his vote was certain:...he at once rose above all infirmities of habit, firm as a rock upon the spiritual foundation on which he rested.[21]

Indeed, what gave Wilberforce peace in these trials of a grueling profession he did not particularly like—"How toilsome and unsatisfactory a path is that of politics!"[22]—was the belief that God judged a person's conscience, not whether he or she always made the correct decisions. After he had studied an issue from both sides, for which he had a gift,[23] and no matter how much he might berate himself before God in his diary for his decisions of the past, he trusted that he could act as a politician, not under the threat of God's condemnation, but under God's mercy. This gave him the confidence and courage that allowed him to wrestle with critical issues, to make mistakes, and to carry on regardless, conscious of God's continuing support and call to serve in the political arena.

On England and the World

Since Wilberforce's theology and spirituality encouraged him to be "useful" as a Christian, since as a politician he was in a position to persuade the passage of critical legislation, and since as a natural leader he was in a position to found or support many social and evangelistic enterprises, it should not be strange if he should have had a pronounced effect on England and the English way of life. Brown claims that there was no true Evangelicalism before Wilberforce and that the true Evangelical Revival was a lay movement led by the eloquent politician:

> Brougham's statement about Wilberforce was right. Before him there was no Evangelicalism…If Wilberforce was the originator of the Bible Society and of the Christian Missionary Society and…thought of Abolition as a part of the reform of England, …it would hardly be possible to doubt that no other man of his day, Wesley included, had so great an effect, for the better or for worse, on the spiritual life of his country.[24]

However, in Chapter II evidence was put forward that Anglican Evangelicalism was in existence many years before Wilberforce's conversion. Brown may be attempting to emphasize that a cohesive Evangelical Movement hardly existed before Wilberforce's leadership, but even this overstates the case—Wilberforce was not the only influential leader of Evangelicalism. It is far wiser to side with Furneaux's statement: "At the time of his [Wilberforce's] conversion, Evangelicalism was a growing movement, and he was able to do much to foster and shape its growth."[25] A large amount of that shaping came from *A Practical View*, the publication of which, according to Houston, "marked the beginning of serious concern for evangelical Christianity among the upper classes in England during the nineteenth century."[26] It was "the most influential manifesto of the Evangelical party"[27] and the influence of that Evangelical party was immense. Henry Perkins writes of its impact, not without criticism:

> Between 1780 and 1850 the English ceased to be one of the most aggressive, brutal, rowdy, outspoken, riotous, cruel and blood-thirsty nations in the world, and became one of the most inhibited, polite, orderly, tender-minded, prudish and hypocritical.[28]

The humanitarian movements of the late eighteenth century, argues Howse, "sprang out of a new doctrine of responsibility toward the unprivileged, a doctrine which received its chief impulse from the Evangelical emphasis on the value of the human soul, and hence, of the individual."[29] Appreciation of the impact of the Evangelical Movement of Wilberforce's day, and of Wilberforce's place as an important leader of the Movement, prompts Pollock to state:

> Wilberforce would disclaim the credit, but the essentials of his beliefs and of his conscience formed the foundation of the British character for the next two generations at least. He was a proof that a man may change his times, though he cannot do it alone.[30]

England was a world power, and what influenced England affected a great deal of the Western and non-Western world, wherever England had its colonies. The slave trade was ended—Wilberforce fought not only for an end to England's trade, but Europe's. Three days before his death he was told that slavery would also end, thanks to his efforts and the efforts of those to whom he entrusted the task at his retirement from politics. Sierra Leone was established thanks to his help. The Bible was spread all over the world because of the British and Foreign Bible Society which he had helped begin, and which spawned sister branches in many countries. He encouraged the Christian missionary movement and thus the widespread promulgation of Christian principles and beliefs. It is a mark of the greatness of the man that he was able to be of such positive influence in the world through his involvement in so many different causes and yet sincerely consider his role in all of these affairs insignificant. He did not spend his final days glorying in what he had been able to accomplish, but in worship of God and in the desire, despite the spiritual poverty he saw within himself, that he be acceptable to God at the end of it all. "With regard to myself," he said two weeks before his death, "I have nothing whatsoever to urge, but the poor Publican's plea, 'God be merciful to me a sinner.'"[31]

Notes

1. Coupland, p. 186.

2. Ibid., pp. 190-1.

3. Furneaux, *Wilberforce*, p. 54.

4. Wilberforce, *A Practical View*, p. ii.

5. Wilberforce, quoted in Wilberforce and Wilberforce, *Life*, 2:21.

6. Ibid., 1:341.

7. Ibid., 3:208-9.

8. Ibid., 3:214.

9. Ibid., 2:69.

10. Ibid., 2:115.

11. Ibid., 2:210.

12. Ibid., 3:154.

13. Ibid., 3:534.

14. Ibid., 4:98.

15. Ibid., 4:190.

16. Ibid., 4:245.

17. Ibid., 4:282.

18. Ibid., 5:46.

19. Ibid., 5:77.

20. Pollock, *Wilberforce*, p. 219.

21. George Stephen, *Anti-Slavery Recollections* (London, 1854), p. 80, cited ibid., pp. 219-20.

22. Wilberforce, quoted in Wilberforce and Wilberforce, *Life*, 3:492.

23. Pollock, *Wilberforce*, p. 218.

24. Brown, p. 529.

25. Furneaux, *Wilberforce*, p. 44.

26. Houston, p. xii.

27. Cragg, p. 155.

28. Henry Perkins, quoted by Lean, p. 83.

29. Howse, p. 7.

30. Pollock, *Wilberforce*, p. 307.

31. Wilberforce, quoted in Wilberforce and Wilberforce, *Life*, 5:364.

CHAPTER VII

The Challenge
Myth and Fact in Wilberforce's Life

William Wilberforce's religious thought created a spirituality that produced an effervescent and Christocentric character which, in its turn, manifested the sort of vision, courage, and perseverance that affected the lives of hundreds of thousands of people, both in Britain and overseas, for the good. Though this biography has not ignored those activities of Wilberforce which people of the twentieth century consider most problematic—his support of repressive legislation and his acceptance of the paternalistic understanding of the inevitable place of the poor in the structure of society—the evidence clearly supports the contention that Wilberforce's Evangelical spirituality moulded a leader whose benevolence and compassion crossed all kinds of boundaries of class and religion and race in order to serve humankind in the name of God and Christ. Yet a great deal of myth has grown up around Wilberforce, myth that tends to cast a pall over his accomplishments. This myth is mainly comprised of four allegations: 1) that Wilberforce cared for the black slaves in the West Indies but did nothing for white British laborers; 2) that Wilberforce only cared for the slaves' physical needs so that he could win them over to the Christian gospel; 3) that Wilberforce involved himself in

Abolition almost exclusively in order to gain recognition for the Evangelical Movement and support for its religious agenda; 4) that Wilberforce and the Evangelicals were culturally impoverished philistines. Each of these allegations will be dealt with in turn.

The idea that Wilberforce fought his whole life for the emancipation of the African slaves, yet never once turned a compassionate eye on the victims of the Industrial Revolution who sprawled at his feet when he stepped from his carriage into the House of Commons, was a belief that grew up during his own generation. One of its main perpetrators was William Cobbett. His infamous attack against Wilberforce's character was unleashed in Cobbett's own paper, *Cobbett's Weekly Political Register*, on August 30, 1823. Its accusations have been reverberating for the past 160 years. Cobbett wrote:

> Wilberforce, I have you before me in a canting pamphlet [An Appeal...in behalf of the Negro Slaves] ...You seem to have a great affection for the fat and lazy and laughing and singing and dancing negros...Never have you done one single act in favour of the labourers of this country...You make your appeal in Piccadilly, London, amongst those who are wallowing in luxuries, proceeding from the labour of the people. You should have gone to the gravel-pits, and made your appeal to the wretched creatures with bits of sacks around their shoulders, and with hay-hands round their legs;...What an insult it is, and what an unfeeling, what a cold-blooded hypocrite must he be that can send it forth; what an insult to call upon people under the name of free British labourers; to appeal to them in behalf of Black slaves, when these free British laboureres; these poor, mocked, degraded wretches, would be happy to lick the dishes and bowls, out of which the Black slaves have breakfasted, dined, or supped.[1]

These are strong words and they have been a strong thread in stitching together the fabric of the myth surrounding Wilberforce. But, as Pollock argues, using the very words Cobbett at one point flung at Wilberforce in his tirade, "Cobbett...as former editor of the

Parliamentary History...must have known [his charge that Wilberforce never helped British labourers] to be a 'cool impudent falsehood' of breathtaking size."[2] This present study of the effects of Wilberforce's spirituality on eighteenth and nineteenth century British society supports Pollock's case against Cobbett's. Twice Wilberforce backed Sir Robert Peel's factory acts, in 1802 and 1812.[3] The Society for Bettering the Condition of the Poor was founded in Wilberforce's house.[4] This Bettering Society—the name it ordinarily went by—in Lean's words, "First called for definite legislation to limit the hours worked by children in the cotton mills, to regulate the age and conditions of apprenticeship and to provide for regular inspection."[5] Wilberforce kept several schools for the poor operating at his personal expense.[6] He and Arthur Young, the eminent English agriculturalist whom Wilberforce led into an Evangelical faith, worked on several methods by which to come up with better and cheaper food for Britain's poor.[7] Nor is this all. This biography has presented many other ways in which Wilberforce assisted the British working class.[8] Yet, unjustly, the caricature of Wilberforce and the Evangelicals of his generation persists, set down in print not only by Cobbett, but by Charles Dickens, as Betty Fladeland notes:

> The old Dickensian stereotype of emancipationists as a collection of Mrs. Jellybys who were oblivious to the fact that exploited white labour at home needed emancipation just as did black slaves in the West Indies...[9]

Wilberforce indeed cared for the people of his own country, but it must be admitted that he still felt that slavery was a worse evil than anything they were being subjected to. Perhaps this attitude of his may have contributed to the caricature. In 1827 he confronted a friend who had compared the situation of the boys used in chimney sweeping, a cause close to Wilberforce's heart, with that of the slaves on British plantations:

> [I was] a little scandalized at your calling their case an evil not less grevious...than that of that Negro slaves. This shows what I have often remarked, that even those who are best informed on

the subject...have frequently a very inadequate idea of its real enormity; for this does not so much consist in extraordinary instances of cruelty as in the habitual immorality and degradation and often grinding sufferings of the poor victims of this wicked system...the systematic misery of their situation.[10]

Considering Wilberforce's obvious distress over the suffering of the slaves, it seems absurd to accuse him, as in the second allegation of the Wilberforce myth, an allegation supported by Brown,[11] of caring for their bodies only in order to be able to get at their souls. This appears to be not only an effort to discredit Wilberforce but also the Evangelical faith that undergirded his convictions. Wilberforce indeed considered the spiritual more important than what was temporal.[12] It would have been inconsistent and hypocritical if Wilberforce, believing this, had not tried to reach the Africans (as well as every other social group) with the gospel that could save their souls for an eternal destiny. But why should this be construed as signifying he cared for the physical needs of the slaves any less, that he did not suffer knowing they suffered? His diaries and letters are peppered with remarks that exhibit his anger over the inhumane situation of the slaves and these remarks are not linked to any sentences on reaching them with the Christian gospel.[13] Even where the religious aims of Wilberforce and the Evangelicals do come through, as they must in those who see the ability to render spiritual benefits to a people as the greater good, this does not erode the case for the Evangelicals' compassion for the suffering of the Africans.

The third allegation, Brown's contention that Wilberforce used Abolition in a calculated move to win popularity, prestige, and influence for the Evangelical Movement,[14] is as nonsensical as the preceding allegation. In April of 1793, soon after Louis XVI's execution in France under the blade of a guillotine, with fears of bloody revolution in England racing through London's streets, Wilberforce wrote a friend: "If I thought the immediate Abolition of the Slave Trade would cause an insurrection in our islands, I should not for an instant remit my most strenuous endeavours."[15] Wilberforce had been an Evangelical Christian for eight years when he said this. If it had leaked out, it was hardly a remark calculated to gain friends in high places or supporters among the conservative and influential elite, persons who could help push for legislation that would allow the gospel to penetrate Britain's colonies. Only one month later Wilberforce would be attempting to get his East India clauses through—even a limited public knowledge of the remark would not have helped him and Wilberforce was not a rash man. The point is, it was no more of a calculated act than Wilberforce's battle to end the slave trade was a calculated act undertaken to serve a hidden agenda. Wilberforce was crying out from the heart in his indignation at the perpetuation of slavery and the slave trade. This sentence was considered too radical, even in 1838, to be printed in Wilberforce's biography. Accordingly, Wilberforce's sons published the letter in which it originally appeared but expunged the inflammatory sentence.[16]

Wilberforce and the Evangelicals got involved in the slave trade because they considered it a great sin and a great evil and in God's name they wanted to remove its curse from Britain's Empire. They fought it, as Ian Bradley asserts, "because they were profoundly moved by human want and suffering."[17] Moreover, it is hard to believe that Wilberforce would have carried on with a cause that lasted twenty years, a cause which was in and out of public and government interest and concern, if all he had cared about was drawing attention to the Evangelical cause. Surely if this was the end desired, there were other popular causes that could have been dealt with in far less time and given the Evangelicals a swifter route to national prominence. And with Abolition accomplished and the Evangelical Movement supposedly where it wished to be in terms of influence, why would Wilberforce and his followers then turn to the equally arduous, painstaking, and lengthy struggle for Emancipation? What purpose could another drawn-out battle possibly serve with respect to Brown's contention? In fact, the Evangelicals took up the cause of Emancipation for the same reason they had taken up the cause of Abolition. Slavery was evil and it was cruel and as humans and Christians they meant to stop it. They were not, states Ervine, "self-seeking in their eagerness for noble patronage, but recognizing the power structure and turning it to 'usefulness.'"[18]

The final allegation, that somehow because they shunned certain amusements and types of literature, Wilberforce and the Evangelicals were cultural iconoclasts, could not be further from the truth. This biography has already argued for the high degree of compatibility the Evangelicals felt with the culture and society of their times.[19] Wilberforce's appreciation of good music and literature and higher education has already been pointed out.[20] It is unfair and inaccurate to lump the Evangelicals and Methodists together in their approaches to the culture of their day. The Evangelical life was not the life of an anchorite. Evangelical Christianity was to work its way through the culture around it like yeast through dough. "No calling," said Wilberforce, "is proscribed, no pursuit is forbidden, no science or art is prohibited, no pleasure is disallowed."[21]

As false as the Wilberforce myth is, however, it will take more than words to dispel it. What will inevitably dissolve the myth will be the reclamation by contemporary Evangelicals within the Anglican Church, as well as evangelicals without it, of the evangelical heritage of that early Movement of Wilberforce's generation. Twenty-first century evangelicalism must pick up where Wilberforce and his followers left off. They must learn to balance personal evangelism with social reform, even the kind of reform that confronts an entire system that is entrenched, popular, and economically viable. They must learn, as Wilberforce learned, to balance solitude with activity, meditation with verbalization, theological education with secular education, seriousness with joy, being Christians with being members of their community and society and culture. The Evangelicalism of Wilberforce's day was known, even if not always appreciated, for its broad range of involvements and concerns: the fight to alter an oppressive criminal code, to employ as well as aid the poor, to transform the conditions in the prisons, to assist agrarian reform, to develop better medical and educational systems. All this was on their agenda along with world evangelization. Such a variety of programs and concerns may exist within some present-day evangelical groups, but these groups are rare and certainly not what contemporary evangelicalism is noted for by the society around it, unlike that first generation of Anglican Evangelicals.

On the Hood River in the Northwest Territories of northern Canada, twenty-five miles south of the Bathurst Inlet and the Arctic Ocean, the highest waterfall above the Arctic Circle drops 160 feet in a cascade of white. The first European to see it was the British explorer John Franklin who was searching for the Northwest Passage. It was the summer of 1821 and Franklin named it Wilberforce Falls.[22]

That torrent which has continued to cut through rock since it was sketched in 1821 by two of Franklin's men is an appropriate symbol for Wilberforce and his Evangelicalism. In his day, his spirituality fed the resolve which cut through much of the immorality and spiritual indifference of Britain. He who became "a moral father to his country"[23] and "the conscience of England"[24] also became a father and a guiding conscience to a spiritual movement that has largely been forgotten. It is critical that the heirs of Wilberforce's legacy, Anglican and non-Anglican, evaluate themselves in light of this vibrant forefather's intense and inclusive spirituality. How much of today's evangelicalism has the purity and breadth and impetus of that first Evangelical Movement and of the largely unhonored layman who was its greatest leader?

Notes

1. William Cobbett, *Cobbett's Weekly Political Register*, 30 Aug. 1823, XLVII cc. 513-16, 520-1, cited by Pollock, *Wilberforce*, p. 287.

2. Pollock, ibid.

3. See Betty Fladeland, *Abolition and Working-Class Problems in the Age of Industrialization* (Baton Rouge: Louisiana State University Press, 1984), p. x.

4. See Lean, p. 144.

5. Ibid.

6. Ibid., p. 153.

7. Ibid.

8. See especially Chapters II and VI.

9. Fladeland, p. viii.

10. Wilberforce, Roberts MSS, letter to S. Roberts, 31 Oct. 1827, cited by Pollock, *Wilberforce*, p. 288.

11. Brown, pp. 380ff.

12. See Chapter IV and Wilberforce, quoted in Wilberforce and Wilberforce, *Life*, 4:126.

13. For examples, see Wilberforce, quoted in Wilberforce and Wilberforce, *Life*, 2:84, 2:139-40, 2:330; 3:213; 5:164.

14. Brown, pp. 380ff.

15. Wilberforce, quoted in Wilberforce and Wilberforce, *Life*, 2:22; for full text, including expunged sentence, see Pollock, *Wilberforce*, p. 123.

16. See Pollock, ibid., pp. xiv and 123.

17. Ian Bradley, *The Call to Seriousness* (New York: Macmillan, 1976), p. 119.

18. Ervine, p. 214.

19. See Chapters II and IV.

20. See Chapter II, the end of Chapter III, and Chapter IV.

21. Wilberforce, *A Practical View*, p. 330.

22. John W. Lentz, "On Canada's Hood River," *National Geographic*, January 1986, p. 138.

23. Furneaux, *Wilberforce*, p. 273.

24. Pollock, *Wilberforce*, p. 220.

Select Bibliography

Anstey, Roger. *The Atlantic Trade and British Abolition 1760-1810.* London: Macmillan, 1975.

Balleine, G.R. *A History of the Evangelical Party in the Church of England.* London: Longmans, Green and Co., 1911.

Baxter, Richard. *The Autobiography of Richard Baxter.* Edited by J.M. Lloyd Thomas. London: J.M. Dent & Sons Ltd., 1931.

_____. *The Practical Works of Richard Baxter.* Edited by W. Orme, 1830; repr. ed., London: George Virtue, 1838.

Bradley, Ian. *The Call to Seriousness.* New York: Macmillan, 1976.

Brown, Ford K. *Fathers of the Victorians.* Cambridge: Cambridge University Press, 1961.

Bull, Josiah. *John Newton.* London: The Religious Tract Society, 1868.

Coupland, Reginald. *The British Anti-Slavery Movement.* London: Thornton Butterworth, Ltd., 1933.

_____. *Wilberforce.* London: Collins, 1923.

Cragg, Gerald R. *The Church and the Age of Reason.* Markham: Penguin, 1960.

Doddridge, Philip. *The Rise and Progress of Religion in the Soul.* 1745; repr. ed., Glasgow: Chalmers & Collins, 1825.

Ervine, William J.C. "Doctrine and Diplomacy: some aspects of the life and thought of the Anglican Evangelical clergy, 1797-1837." Ph.D. thesis, University of Cambridge, 1979.

Fieling, Keith. *A History of England.* London: Macmillan, 1950.

Fladeland, Betty. *Abolitionists and Working-Class Problems in the Age of Industrialization.* Baton Rouge: Louisiana State University Press, 1984.

Forster, E.M. *Marianne Thornton.* London: Arnold, 1956.

Furneaux, Robin. Foreword to *Journey to the Lake District from Cambridge* (1779), by William Wilberforce. Stocksfield: Oriel Press, 1983.

_____. *William Wilberforce.* London: Hamish Hamilton, 1974.

Hall, Walter P. and Albion, Robert G. *A History of England and the British Empire.* London: Ginn & Co., 1937.

Halevy, Elie. *A History of the English People in 1815.* New York: Harcourt, Brace & Co., 1924.

_____. *A History of the English People 1815-30.* London: T. Fisher Unwin Ltd., 1926.

Haller, William. *The Rise of Puritanism.* Philadelphia: University of Pennsylvania Press, 1938.

Heeney, Brian. *A Different Kind of Gentleman.* Hamden: Archon Books, 1976.

Hennell, Michael, *John Venn and the Clapham Sect.* London: Lutterworth Press, 1958.

Hopkins, Hugh Evan. *Charles Simeon of Cambridge.* Grand Rapids: Eerdmans, 1977.

Hopkins, Mary Alden. *Hannah More and Her Circle.* Toronto: Longmans, Green and Co., 1947.

Howse, Ernest Marshall. *Saints in Politics.* Toronto: University of Toronto, 1952.

Jay, Elisabeth. *The Religion of the Heart*. Oxford: Clarendon Press, 1979.

Jay, William. *The Autobiography of William Jay*. Edited by George Redford and John Angell James. 1854; repr. ed., Edinburgh: The Banner of Truth Trust, 1974.

Johnson, Paul. *A History of Christianity*. Weidenfeld and Nicolson, 1976; repr ed., Markham: Pelican, 1980.

Jones, M.G. *Hannah More*. New York: Greenwood Press, 1968.

Keeble, N.H. *Richard Baxter*. Oxford: Clarendon Press, 1982.

Ladell, A.R. *Richard Baxter*. London: SPCK, 1925.

Lean, Garth. *God's Politician*. London: Darton, Longman and Todd, 1980.

Lewis, Donald Munro. "The Evangelical Mission to the British Working Class: A Study of the growth of Anglican support for a pan-evangelical approach to evangelism, with special reference to London, 1828-1860." Ph.D. thesis, University of Oxford, 1981.

Lewis, Peter. *The Genius of Puritanism*. Haywards Heath: Carey Publications, 1975.

Lockhart, J.G. *The Peacemakers (1814-15)*. London: Duckworth, 1932.

Martin, Bernard. *John Newton*. London: Heinemann, 1950.

Martin, Hugh. *Puritanism and Richard Baxter*. London: SCM Press Ltd., 1954.

Meacham, Standish. *Henry Thornton of Clapham*. Cambridge: Harvard University Press, 1964.

Monk, Robert C. *John Wesley: His Puritan Heritage*. Nashville: Abingdon Press, 1966.

Newton, John. *The Life of the Reverend John Newton*. London: The Religious Tract Society, n.d.

_____. *The Works of John Newton*. London: Thomas Nelson, 1849.

Nuttall, Geoffrey F., ed. *Philip Doddridge*. London: Independent Press Ltd., 1951.

_____. *Richard Baxter and Philip Doddridge*. London: Oxford University Press, 1951.

_____. *Richard Baxter*. London: Thomas Nelson, 1965.

Owen, John. *The Works of John Owen*. Edited by William H. Goold. Vols. 6 and 7. New York: Robert Carter and Brothers, 1852.

Pollock, John. *Amazing Grace*. San Francisco: Harper & Row, 1981.

_____. *Wilberforce*. London: Constable, 1977.

Powicke, Frederick J. *A Life of the Rev. Richard Baxter*. London: Jonathan Cape Ltd., 1924.

_____. *The Rev. Richard Baxter Under the Cross*. London: Jonathan Cape Ltd., 1927.

Rosman, Doreen. *Evangelicals and Culture*. London and Canberra: Croom Helm, 1984.

Russell, George W.E. *The Household of Faith*. London: Mowbray, 1906.

Stephen, Leslie and Lee, Sidney, eds., *The Dictionary of National Biography*. 1949-50 ed., London: Oxford University Press.

Vidler, Alec R. *The Church in an Age of Revolution*. Markham: Penguin, 1961.

Wakefield, Gordon S., ed., *The Westminster Dictionary of Christian Spirituality*. Philadelphia: The Westminster Press, 1983.

Walvin, James, ed., *Slavery and British Society 1776-1846*. London: The Macmillan Press Ltd., 1982.

Warner, Oliver. *William Wilberforce*. London: B.T. Batsford Ltd., 1962.

Wigley, John. *The Rise and Fall of the Victorian Sunday*. Manchester: University Press, 1980.

Wilberforce, Robert Isaac and Wilberforce, Samuel. *The Correspondence of William Wilberforce*, 2 vols. London: John Murray, 1840.

_____. *The Life of William Wilberforce*, 5 vols. London: John Murray, 1838.

Wilberforce, William. *A Practical View of the Prevailing Religious System of Professed Christians, in the Higher and Middle Classes in this*

Country, Contrasted with Real Christianity. 1797; repr. ed., Edinburgh: Johnstone and Hunter, n.d.

_____. *An Appeal to the Religion, Justice and Humanity of the British Empire in behalf of the Negro Slaves in the West Indies*. 1823; repr. ed., New York: Negro University's Press, 1969.

Important Dates
in Wilberforce's Life

1759   Born in Hull, England

1780   First elected to Parliament (Hull)

1784   Second election to Parliament (Yorkshire)

1785   Converted to Christianity

1789   Makes his first motion in Parliament for the abolition of
       the slave trade

1797   Marries Barbara Spooner and publishes his book,
       A Practical View

1807   The slave trade is abolished

1818   Begins to take up the cause of the Abolition of Slavery

1821   Due to ill health offers the leadership of the Anti-Slavery
       campaign to Evangelical MP Thomas Fowell Buxton

1825   Retires from Parliament

1830   Chairs a meeting of the Anti-Slavery Society for the final time

1833   Hears that the third reading of the Bill for the Abolition of Slavery has been passed on July 26 and dies on July 29; buried at Westminster Abbey

1834   One year after Wilberforce's death, at midnight on July 31, 800,000 slaves are freed as the institution of slavery ceases to exist in the British territories.

OTHER BOOKS
OF
INTEREST

"An easy and absorbing read...
Quite a man. Quite a heart. Quite a book."
The Mercury

DAVID
LIVINGSTONE
THE TRUTH BEHIND THE LEGEND
Rob Mackenzie

DAVID LIVINGSTONE
The truth behind the legend
Rob Mackenzie

An easy and absorbing read… Quite a man. Quite a heart. Quite a book.
The Mercury

A man of whom the human race can be justly proud. He shows us that courage, determination and faith are more than a match for life's great challenges.
Bob Edmiston, Chairman, International Motors Group

Livingstone, perhaps the best known missionary of them all. The story of a poor lad from Scotland whose attempts to find the source of the Nile and famous meeting with Henry Morton Stanley have become the stuff of legend.

The truth behind the legend, however, is even more compelling. Drawing extensively from Livingstone's personal notes and letters, Rob Mackenzie unfolds the intensely human story of a man with a vision – to set souls free from slavery, both physically and spiritually, and to open up Africa to Christianity and lawful commerce.

What caused him to become such a well-loved figure, and to attempt such immense tasks?

An amazing story awaits you upon turning the first page

ISBN 1 85792 615 3

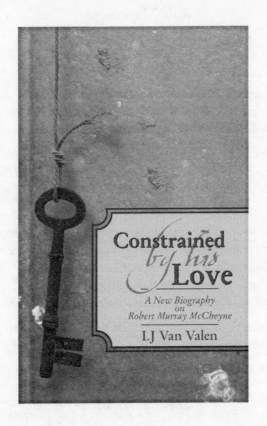

Constrained
by his
Love

*A New Biography
on
Robert Murray McCheyne*

LJ Van Valen

CONSTRAINED BY HIS LOVE
A New Biography on Robert Murray McCheyne
LJ Van Valen

Robert Murray McCheyne was born in 1813 and died, aged 29 in 1843. His life was nothing short of extraordinary. Given the charge of St Peter's Church, Dundee at the tender age of 23, even his trial sermon was blessed, with two people being saved. Soon the church was overflowing with 1,100 hearers, more than a quarter of the local population.

It was not just his preaching that marked him out from the crowd. His spirituality, and focus on the work of Christ was immediately apparent – with hostile crowds melting as they realised the sincerity of the man and the power of his message. Suffering from a range of illnesses his short life is a lesson to us all. When we submit to our Sovereign Lord and his plan, he will use us, no matter how weak we are.

A wonderful example of a servant of God, who denied himself totally in winning souls for Christ.

Finally—a definitive, contemporary biography on Robert Murray M'Cheyne abounding with historical detail, sterling illustrations, and spiritual warmth'

Dr. Joel R. Beeke
President of Puritan Reformed Theological Seminary
Grand Rapids, Michigan

He was an outstanding man of God, and his life story, here told in fullest detail and with fullest sympathy, should on no account be missed.

Dr. J. I. Packer
Professor of Systematic and Historical Theology,
Regent College, Vancouver

ISBN 1 85792 793 1

'Newton's friends and opponents come alive'
John Pollock

AUTHORISED BIOGRAPHY

John
NEWTON

RICHARD CECIL AUGMENTED BY
MARYLYNN ROUSE

THE LIFE OF JOHN NEWTON
Richard Cecil
Edited by Marylynn Rousse

The author of Amazing Grace and many other famous hymns was one of the best loved and most influential of the early evangelicals. His story was extraordinary. A sailor who was flogged for desertion, afterwards a slave in West Africa in all but name and then when rescued, a slave trader. He was converted in a great storm at sea. Although his path to assurance and service was slow, the ex-slaver, ex-lecher, ex-atheist became a true minister of the gospel and a doughty ally of William Wilberforce in the abolition of the slave trade.

Richard Cecil was his first biographer. Cecil had known 'Mr N.', as he calls him, in his later years and the book became a classic. It has long been out of print. Marylynn Rousse has done a good service in editing a new edition but she has done far more. She has found out a great deal about Newton which Cecil did not know so that he becomes a fully rounded figure, and just as loveable.

Wisely, Marylynn does not splatter Cecil's pages with footnotes or insertions, so the reader gets the full flavour of Cecil's prose....Instead, she adds an appendix to each chapter, writing much new material from her very thorough researches. Newton's friends and opponents come alive. Passages in poems of Wordsworth, Coleridge, and of course Cowper, which Newton inspired are brought to hand. Marylynn has also discovered unpublished letters and other treasures and she adds a most useful Who's Who.

John Pollock

ISBN 1 85792 284 0

A New Biography of
HUDSON TAYLOR

IT IS NOT
DEATH
TO DIE

Jim Cromarty

It is Not Death to Die
A New biography of Hudson Taylor
Jim Cromarty

Hudson Taylor's philosophy was simple

> 'There is a living God,
> He has spoken in the Bible.
> He means what he says,
> and will do all that he has promised.'

Hudson Taylor's life is one that should encourage Christians to step out in faith to fulfil the commands of God. His life's work was motivated by a love of God and a love of his fellow man. His heart's desire was to see Christ glorified in people coming to faith, particularly the Chinese.

Encouraged by another missionary, W.C. Burns, Hudson changed western dress and imperialistic attitudes for Chinese ways. He served, and still serves, as a model for mission work around the world.

He led an extraordinary life and Jim Cromarty has succeeded in capturing the thrill of his pioneering work. It is as if we too are able to step outside the comfortable boundaries most of us never come close to exploring beyond.

Jim Cromarty is an Australian minister and has written other respected biographies and family devotional books.

ISBN 1 85792 632 3

CHRISTIAN FOCUS PUBLICATIONS

We publish books for all ages.

STAYING FAITHFUL

In dependence upon God we seek to help make his infallible word, the Bible, relevant. Our aim is to ensure that the Lord Jesus Christ is presented as the only hope to obtain forgiveness of sin, live a useful life, and look forward to heaven with him.

REACHING OUT

Christ's last command requires us to reach out to our world with his gospel. We seek to help fulfil that by publishing books that point people towards Jesus and for them to develop a Christ-like maturity. We aim to equip all levels of readers for life, work, ministry and mission.

Books in our adult range are published in three imprints:-

Christian Focus contains popular works including biographies, commentaries, basic doctrine, and Christian living. Our children's books are also published in this imprint.

Christian Heritage contains classic writings from the past.

Mentor focuses on books written at a level suitable for Bible College and seminary students, pastors, and other serious readers; the imprint includes commentaries, doctrinal studies, examination of current issues, and church history.

Christian Focus Publications, Ltd
Geanies House, Fearn, Ross-shire,
IV20 1TW, Scotland, United Kingdom
info@christianfocus.com

www.christianfocus.com